Contents

Document

Skip Norman: *On Africa* – Script: p. 3

Material

The last letter from Patrice Lumumba to his wife, shortly before his murder in January 1961: p. 21

Commentary

Sónia Vaz Borges: Reconstructing Fragments for the Future of Liberation: p. 23

Volker Pantenburg: Africa from Berlin: p. 24

Tom Holert: Hidden Persuader: p. 25

Madeleine Bernstorff: Paratexts / (Retroactive) Scripts
Or "The last letter from Patrice Lumumba to his wife answers all skeptical questions.": p. 27

Marie-Hélène Gutberlet: Patterns of Improvisation: p. 29

Editorial Note: p. 31

Imprint/Acknowledgments: p. 32

kamera
Resa Dabui
Carlos Bustamante
Skip Norman

musik
Billy Brooks

co-produktion
Denso Film
Pan African Arts Co-Op

regie
Skip Norman

On Africa
by Skip Norman

The documentary film *On Africa*, a co-production of Pan-African Arts CO-OP and Denso Film Berlin by Skip Norman and his friend Joey Gibbs (script), is about the African liberation struggles being fought in Africa today.

The starting point of this film is the relationship between Europe's prosperity and Africa's poverty; Europe's destruction of societies and cultures, and the simultaneous use of Christianity and racial theories as justification for the massive exploitation of the colonized.

Through a dynamic combination of film technique and partisan sensibility in dealing with the facts, it shows the strength and weakness of Europe as a result of the colonial age: the weakness and strength of Africa as proof of Africa's rebirth.

The case of Angola shows the European opinion regarding the liberation of Africa, especially the liberation struggles in the Portuguese territories.

Today, it is clearly visible to everyone how the European colonialists established their rule in Africa.
It is clear to everyone that the Western capitalist system, through the manipulation of industrial and financial capital, is impeding Africa's progress.

"The imperialists have two main goals in Africa:

1) To ensure that the countries that gained independence remain under imperialist domination.

2) To consolidate Portugal and South Africa's inhuman exploitation of the population and resources of Southern Africa and to use these territories as a bulwark of white rule in Africa."

In the film, the armed struggle appears as the real struggle. MPLA in Angola, FRELIMO in Mozambique, PAIGC in Guinea (Bissau), ZAPU in Zimbabwe (Southern Rhodesia), ANC in Azania (South Africa), and SWAPO in Namibia (South West Africa) show that the armed struggle liberates the souls and energy of the people.

The last letter from Patrice Lumumba to his wife answers all skeptical questions.

Document

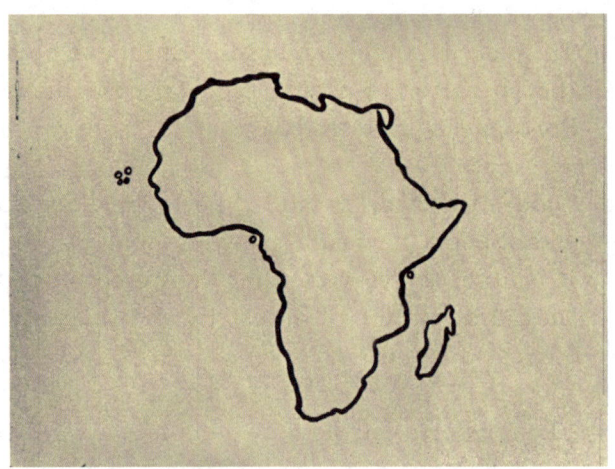

Document

Introduction: Voice 1

In Africa, there are two types of climate: equatorial and tropical.

Tracking shot passing pedestrians (negative effect)

Besides these, there are also several small distinctive climate zones.

Central Africa, Guinea, and East Africa belong to the equatorial climate.

In Guinea and East Africa, there is constant warmth and little precipitation.

Both in the equatorial and tropical climate there is rich vegetation.

The East African climate is hot. There is savannah and diverse vegetation.

The tropical climate is divided into the Sudanese type of heat, temperature fluctuations between day and night, and little rainfall.

There is also the typical Mediterranean climate with hot summers and rain in winter. And the climate of the Cape area is characterized by milder summers and winters and little precipitation.

(tropical sound)

Voice 2

Africa map I (white – black)

Africa's earth is rich. However, its products do not enrich Africans, but mainly groups and individuals still working towards Africa's impoverishment.

With a population of around 280 million people, about 8 % of the world's population, Africa has a share of only 2 % of the total global production.

Continuation of tracking shot

Africa's iron reserves are estimated to be twice as high as those of the U.S.A. and 2/3 of those of the Soviet Union.

Africa's estimated coal reserves will last for 300 years.

New oil deposits are found and exploited all over the continent. But the processing of the most important ores and minerals is only in the early stages.

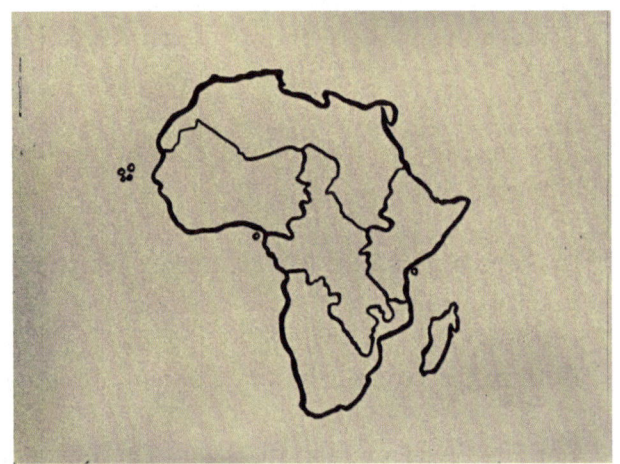

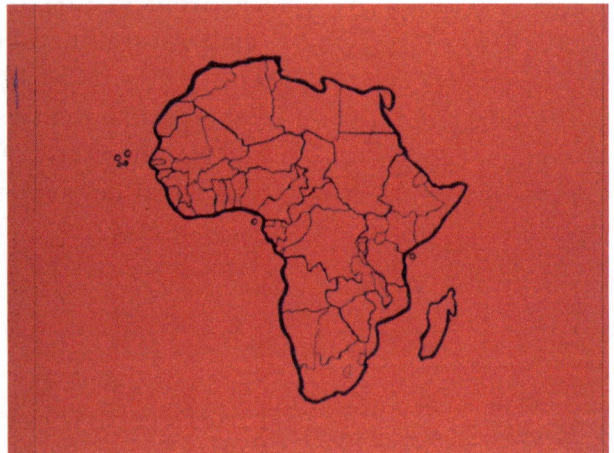

Africa possesses more than 40 % of the world's potential hydro-electric power, a larger share than any other continent. Yet not even 5 % of this is used.

(sound of marching soldiers)

Despite vast stretches of desert in the Sahara, Africa still has more farmland and grazing land than the U.S.A. or the Soviet Union or Asia.

Africa map II
(pink – black)

Africa has twice as much forest as the U.S.A.

Voice 3

Tracking shot
continued

If Africa's diverse riches are used for its own development, it can count among the most modern continents in the world. Its resources have been and continue to be used for the greater development of foreign interests.

By the time Europe recognized Africa in all its magnitude, strength, and power, Africa had long since conceived of itself in this way. It had developed its own forms of government and social organizations that were firmly rooted in its tradition and characterized by its diversity.

Africa map III
(red – black)
dismemberment
of Africa

At that time, the world consisted of many isolated cultures that developed according to their own dynamics. Up until Europe went beyond its borders and left behind a flood of blood and immeasurable destruction.

(war sounds)

IMPERIALISM   Voice 2

Europe at home
and in Africa –
aristocracy –
military

Imperialism is the practice of a stronger country imposing its will on another country by military force in order to achieve the economic and political domination of that people.

REPEAT: Voice 1

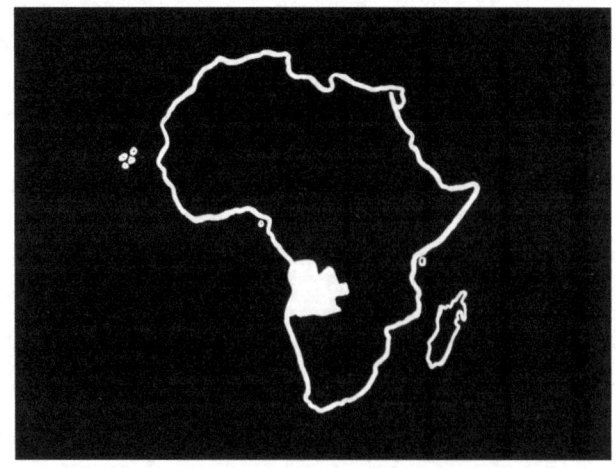

Voice 3

<u>Imperialism</u> – Europe's spread of capitalist exploitation and dissemination of Christianity and racial theories over more than half of humanity.

REPEAT: Voice 1

Voice 3

<u>Imperialism</u> – Europe's inhuman invention of concentration camps, mass mutilation and mass murder, desecration of women, gruesome treatment of children, the destruction of cultures all over the world.

Voice 1

<u>Imperialism</u> – Europe's inhuman invention of concentration camps, mass mutilation and mass murder, desecration of women, gruesome treatment of children, the destruction of cultures all over the world, all in the name and for the defense of a racial theory. With a supremacy principle of European Christian civilization, which feels destined to rule the world.

Voice 3

Europeans in Africa

After Europe had discovered its so-called "New World," it introduced the fatal system of permanent slavery. A new doctrine of labor emerged. People were divided into two classes: the master men and the subhumans; the master men were the real men, the subhumans, however, only half-men or even less.

(church scene)

Slavery

Thus began the first invasion, the first destruction and devastation of Africa, the basis for the development of capitalism in Europe.

What is Angola?   Voice 1

Africa map IV
(black – white)

Angola is: the largest African coffee producer and ranks third in world production

the second largest African producer of fish meal and fish oil and ranks tenth in the world producer list

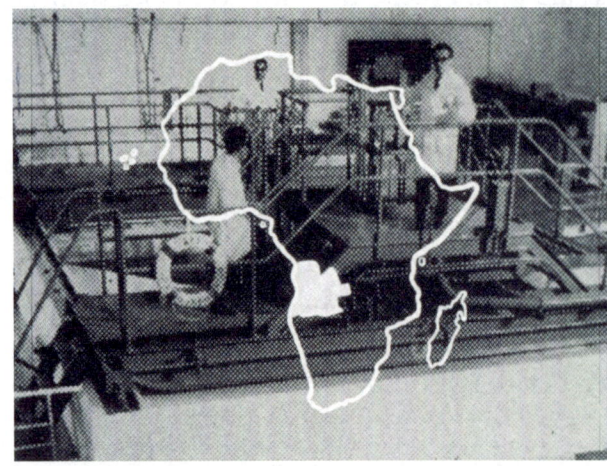 

	the second largest producer of sisal in Africa
	in fifth place of oil production in Africa
Photomontage of Portuguese prosperity compared to Angola (didactics)	will take a place among the top three in a few years
	in sixth place in African tobacco production
	the largest African paper producer
	the second largest producer of diamonds on the African continent
	Africa's second largest ore supplier, ranking twelfth in world production.

<u>Voice 2</u>

Portuguese prosperity

Portugal practices the most extreme and primitive form of exploitation that exists in Africa.
According to the labor law for indigenous people, which was passed in 1828 and is for the most part still in effect today, six forms of exploitation of indigenous labor in the Portuguese colonies can be distinguished.

1) FORCED LABOR in cases of a violation of punishment or labor laws, e.g. non-payment of head tax.

2) OBLIGATORY WORK that can be imposed on anyone if there aren't enough workers available for public works. Exception: children under 14 years of age, adults over 60 years of age, sick and disabled people, recognized chiefs, Africans in permanent employment.

3) CONTRACTUAL WORK as the economically most important form of forced labor in the Portuguese colonies. Any African who is unable to prove that he has been in employment for at least 6 months of the previous year can be used for forced labor for the state or for private entrepreneurs.

4) VOLUNTARY WORK, in which workers sign a contract directly with the entrepreneur, the only advantage of which over contractual work is that African workers are guaranteed a job close to their village. Wages for voluntary work are on average even lower than those for contractual work.

5) FORCED CULTIVATION of cotton. In northern Mozambique, twelve companies, which have a monopoly in the area, require African farmers to grow cotton. The company has to sell it at fixed prices, which are lower than those of the free market. No other work is allowed in the concessionary areas.

This deprives the African farmers of their livelihood, their subsistence economy. The result is frequent famines.

6) MIGRANT WORK, which has existed in the form of an agreement between Mozambique and Transvaal since 1909, and which represents a special form of forced labor. The monopoly on recruiting migrant workers is in the hands of the Witwatersrand Native Labour Association, which pays the Portuguese government 1 pound 18 shillings per worker.

The result: an intensive exploitation of Africa through slave trading in order to exploit a gigantic workforce for Europe's production and social progress.

Voice 3

Europe 1800

Europe applied its policy of Balkanization to Africa. Africa was of such great value to Europe that wars on the European continent had to be waged because of Africa. Peoples and territories changed owners like children changed their toys.

Thus, the great Berlin Conference of the imperialists and colonialists was held between November 1884 and January 1885 to find solutions for the division of territories along the Atlantic coast and in Central Africa.

It caused conflicts between the European states, which led to the dismemberment of Africa into spheres of influence of the European nations.

In 1890, the German and English spheres of influence were defined and the way was cleared for a stronger invasion as well as an intensified exploitation of the mineral resources in the Congolian lowlands and the large mineral deposits further south.

(image)

Document

| | COLONIALISM | Voice 1 |

Documentation of colonialism

Colonialism – the subjugation of territories and peoples through military occupation in order to extract mineral resources and acquire the products of labor. These territories serve as labor markets for the industrial products coming from the colonizers.

(image)

Voice 2

Under the politics of colonialism, the colonized people are seen as mere tools. They are forced to live in extreme poverty and have no right to self-government. They also have no control over the distribution of the products of their labor.

(image)

The result –
> Extreme poverty in the colonies was the basis of wealth and luxury in Europe.

(image)

NEO-COLONIALISM   Voice 1

Neo-colonialism is the control over formally independent states by groups of big financial capital. These groups are supported by imperialist governments.

(image)

Voice 3

Statistical data

In 1957, Africa supplied Europe with the following quantity of raw materials for its industries.

Voice 3

Documentary images

The U.S.A. is one of the main representatives of neo-colonialism. Between 1950 and 1959, private American companies invested $4.5 billion in developing countries. They made a profit that was three times greater than their investments. Net profits were $8.3 billion, plus millions in trade profits, interest on bonds, freight charges, and profits from other businesses.

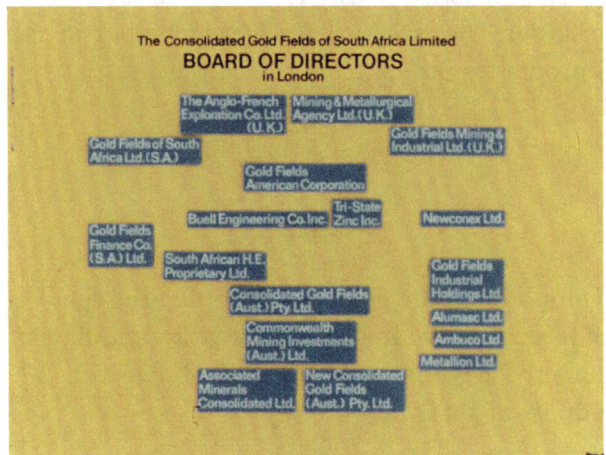 

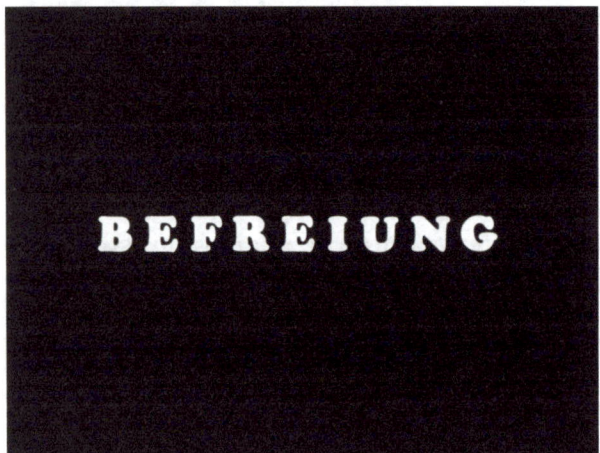 

Document

	Voice 1
Documentation of neo-colonialism	One of the imperialists' most effective methods of maintaining economic rule over the former colonial areas is to try to keep the young states restricted in the monetary zones of the imperialist financial centers. There are 7 major currency groups in Africa: the French franc zone, the English sterling zone, the Belgian franc zone, the Spanish peseta zone, the Portuguese escudo zone, and other countries such as the United Arab Republic and Congo (Kinshasa) with other currency units. Most of the trade in Africa is in the sterling zone and the French franc zone.
	The existence of individual monetary zones has a detrimental effect on the growth of trade in Africa, leading to illegal trade and loss of income in many countries. It prevents the establishment of an African Economic Community. These monetary zones maintain the links with the former colonial powers and strengthen the forces of neo-colonialism.
	Voice 2
	Another method of neo-colonialism is the use of high interest rates. World Bank figures from 1962 show that 71 countries from Asia, Africa, and Latin America had about $27 billion foreign debts, for which they also had to pay about $5 billion in interest and services fees.
	Voice 3
Photomontage metropolis – colonial city	In 1961, for example, the profit from international aid was $5 billion, from interest $1 billion, and from non-equivalent exchange $5.8 billion – a total of $11.8 billion won in exchange for an investment of $6 billion. So "aid" is nothing more than another method of exploitation, a modern method of capitalist export – only by a different name.
	LIBERATION Voice 3
The freedom movement: training, education, production	The "return of the African peoples to history" presupposes the liberation of the development process of the national productive forces from any kind of imperialist domination, and this cannot be achieved through negotiation or compromise, but only by revolutionary struggle.

Document

<u>Voice 1</u>

No country in Africa became independent without victims.
All concessions made by the imperialists were forced through the
actions of the masses. No country was granted independence.

The imperialists have two main goals in Africa:

1) To ensure that the countries that gained independence remain
under imperialist domination.

2) To consolidate Portugal and South Africa's inhuman exploitation
of the population and resources of Southern Africa and to use
these territories as a bulwark of white rule in Africa.

<u>Voice 2</u>

Africa is land. The struggle to improve agriculture and rural development will determine the future of the continent and its individual nations.

It is necessary to determine and establish the exact proportions
of both agricultural and industrial development.

Industrialization must be connected with the needs and possibilities
of one's own economy and cannot be done in order to satisfy the
European societies. It cannot be guided by the principles resulting
from the materialistic societies of the industrial superpowers.

```
FRELIMO ----------- MOZAMBIQUE
MPLA --------------- ANGOLA
PAIGC -------------- GUINEA BISSAU
SWAPO -------------- SOUTH WEST AFRICA
ANC ---------------- SOUTH AFRICA
ZAPU --------------- ZIMBABWE
```

Document

The last letter from Patrice Lumumba to his wife, shortly before his murder in January 1961.

My dear wife,

I am writing these words not knowing whether they will reach you, when they will reach you, and whether I shall still be alive when you read them. All through my struggle for the independence of my country, I have never doubted for a single instant the final triumph of the sacred cause to which my companions and I have devoted all of our lives. But what we wished for our country, its right to an honorable life, to unstained dignity, to independence without restrictions, was never desired by the Belgian imperialists and their Western allies, who found direct and indirect support, both deliberate and unintentional, amongst certain high officials of the United Nations, that organization in which we placed all our trust when we called on its assistance.

They have corrupted some of our compatriots and bribed others. They have helped to distort the truth and bring our independence into dishonor. How could I speak otherwise? Dead or alive, free or in prison by order of the imperialists, it is not myself who counts. It is the Congo, it is our poor people for whom independence has been transformed into a cage from whose confines the outside world looks on us, sometimes with kindly sympathy, but at other times with joy and pleasure.

But my faith will remain unshakeable. I know and I feel in my heart that sooner or later my people will rid themselves of all their enemies, both internal and external, and that they will rise as one man to say "No" to the degradation and shame of colonialism, and regain their dignity in the clear light of the sun. We are not alone. Africa, Asia and the free liberated people from all corners of the world will always be found at the side of the millions of Congolese who will not abandon the struggle until the day when there are no longer any colonialists and their mercenaries in our country. As to my children whom I leave and whom I may never see again, I should like them to be told that the future of the Congo is beautiful, and that their country expects them, as it expects every Congolese, to fulfill the sacred task of rebuilding our independence and our sovereignty; for without dignity there is no liberty, without justice there is no dignity, and without independence there are no free men.

Neither brutality, nor cruelty nor torture will ever bring me to ask for mercy, for I prefer to die with my head unbowed, my faith unshakable and with profound trust in the destiny of my country, rather than live under subjection and disregarding sacred principles. History will one day have its say, but it will not be the history that is taught in Brussels, Paris, Washington or in the United Nations but the history which will be taught in the countries freed from imperialism and its puppets. Africa will write its own history, and to the north and south of the Sahara, it will be a glorious and dignified history.

Do not weep for me, my dear wife. I know that my country, which is suffering so much, will know how to defend its independence and its liberty.

Long live the Congo! Long live Africa!

Patrice

Reconstructing Fragments for the Future of Liberation

In "Further Considerations on Afrofuturism," Kodwo Eshun speculates on a future generation of African archaeologists excavating a site from the past era. They encounter ruined documents belonging to our present, and wonder incites us to "imagine them reconstructing the conceptual framework of our cultural moment from those fragments."[1]

Watching Skip Norman's *On Africa* allows us to think that the future which, Eshun asks us to imagine, is a time ahead of us, yet can also be inherited from the past. The thirty-six minutes of film confront us with an assemblage of images and sounds that does not necessarily follow a historical chronology, but produces futurities, provides a platform for departure.

The last words of Democratic Republic of Congo's first Prime Minister Patrice Lumumba (1925–61), in a letter to Pauline Lumumba and their kids (but it might as well be addressed to all Africans and the diaspora), predict a specific African future: "History will one day have its say, but it will not be the history that is taught in Brussels, Paris, Washington or in the United Nations but the history which will be taught in the countries freed from imperialism and its puppets. Africa will write its own history, and to the north and south of the Sahara, it will be a glorious and dignified history."

Such "right to an honorable life, to unstained dignity, to independence without restrictions," was already in the making thanks to collectives and internationalist movements on the continent. FRELIMO in Mozambique; SWAPO in Namibia; PAIGC in Guinea Bissau and Cabo Verde; MPLA in Angola; ANC in South Africa and ZAPU in Zimbabwe, are some of the organizations that Norman evokes to introduce us to the geographies of liberation against imperialism, capitalism, colonialism, and neocolonialism.

The liberation struggle represents a collective struggle, the goal of which exceeds independence. It is an individual/collective, processal response of the people as they become conscious of the racialization, dehumanization, oppression, and exploitation through which they are subjugated under colonial-oppressive government inside and outside their "country." They organize themselves to dismantle and destroy the structure of oppression, to build their sovereignty and "justice and dignity" as free men, for whom independence, in the words of Lumumba, is a crucial passage to the liberation of the future.

Such a vision of a liberated future of Africa and Africans, cannot be created without demonstrating how the geographies of oppression dominate the world space, and how they are propagated and developed throughout times and places, revealing an international network of violence and dehumanization. It is through currency and the seven monetary zones in Africa that the links with former colonial powers are perpetuated. Starting in minute 21.53, in the chapter on "neo-colonialism," Norman demonstrates how the structure of colonialism and imperialism developed in an almost untraceable structure, which prevents the establishment of an African Economic Community, or if we might use Eshun's Afrofuturistic vision, the United States of Africa—USAF.

More than a schematic form of presenting this structure, Norman associates sounds with visual effects: slide images of banks pass in a fast-paced sequence. The rhythm is associated with clicking sounds, reminiscent of a bill counting machine or a cash register, combined with the ticking of a clock. By establishing such associations between sound and image, Norman leads us into thinking that the process of counting money keeps going, relentlessly, just like time.

The images that follow echo and contrast with the first scene of the film, where we see passersby rendered in black and white

---

[1] Kodwo Eshun, "Further Considerations on Afrofuturism," in *CR: The New Centennial Review*, vol. 3, no. 2, (Summer 2003): 287–302, here 287.

negative in a modern city. Now, Norman shows the other side of the coin by choosing to show the faces and the landscape of dilapidated places in Africa, creating a clear image of those affected by the exploitation that finances the lifestyle of those in the Global North, in this case in the streets of West Berlin.

Neocolonialism is not limited to the African continent. It expands to Asia and Latin American, often disguised as "aid." Again, Norman intersects neocolonialism with Lumumba's last letter proclaiming the international fight for liberation: "We are not alone. Africa, Asia and the free liberated peoples from all corners of the globe will always be found at the side of the millions of Congolese who will not abandon the struggle."

Norman's assemblage of "countermemories"[2] and his lesson about liberation and its obstacles, composed of fragmented images and sounds, reminds us of Eshun's excavation site, of the place from where the liberation struggles can be thought about. It is a powerful visual lesson on what needs to be done to continue the work that liberation movements across the globe struggle for on a daily basis.

"No country in Africa became independent without victims (and) no country was granted independence." These remarks in On Africa open the chapter on "liberation" ("Befreiung"). Guided by the sound of explosions and gunshots, Norman transports us to the stage of liberation war, a path that many movements chose to follow in their struggle to achieve the goals set in the fight against colonialism. The closing images of the film are of Moise Tshombe (1919–69) and Patrice Lumumba, the first personifying the destruction of Congo and alliance with colonial powers, and the latter, the "caged" and murdered by colonial forces. It is the heartbeat that accompanies Lumumba's letter, featuring his last words: "Long live Africa!"

Sónia Vaz Borges

---

2   Ibid., 288.

Africa from Berlin

The title is clear: this is a film about Africa—the continent, its history of exploitation and violence and its decolonial struggle. At the same time, On Africa is a film about West Berlin, the city where Skip Norman had moved in 1966. The first images we see are black and white traveling shots of Kurfürstendamm. They are rendered in negative so that the white people in the streets appear Black. The tracking shot registers the shops and cafés, the banking houses, the department store Kaufhaus des Westens, the abundance of the consumer world. In the voice-over, one of the two female voices points to the economic basis of this wealth: "Africa's earth is rich," she says. "Its products do not enrich Africans, but mainly groups and individuals still working towards Africa's impoverishment." From the start, we are confronted with a gap between image and sound. This gap structurally hints at the asymmetry between the colonial powers and their victims. The film often uses such contrasts in its didactic impetus, between what is said and what is seen.

Seventeen minutes into the film, following a sober assessment of the extractivist exploitation of the continent, we return to Berlin. This time the Berlin of 1884. Black and white photographs show a luxurious building, the Reichskanzlerpalais also known as "Alte Reichskanzlei." It no longer exists today, but back then it was located in Wilhelmstraße, not far from the location of the Deutsche Film- und Fernsehakademie Berlin (DFFB) at Potsdamer Platz today. Between November 15, 1884 and February 26, 1885, the colonial powers of Europe convened here for the infamous "Kongo-Konferenz" to dissect the African continent into zones of influence. Skip Norman's film revisits this event as one of the primal scenes of colonial violence; what's more, it is the political event where the two driving forces of the West, colonialism and imperialism, can be studied in perfect coalescence. Midway between the brutal conquest of the continent in the fifteenth and sixteenth centuries and the contemporary politics of development in around 1970, Berlin is at the center of the carefully planned and executed oppression of Africa's indigenous population.

Apart from the images of consumerism and exploitation highlighted by Kurfürstendamm, and the focus on one of the primal scenes of European violence in 1884/85, there is the specific background of DFFB. Skip Norman had graduated from the school in 1969 with *Strange Fruit*. Formally, he was no longer a student when he realized *On Africa*. However, the voices in the film point to the school context. The male voice belongs to Klaus Wildenhahn, the most important protagonist of "direct cinema" in Germany. Wildenhahn had started to teach at DFFB after the turmoil of 1967/68 that culminated in the expulsion of eighteen students. Thanks to Wildenhahn's efforts, a new sense of community emerged with collective projects such as the political newsreel series "Wochenschau." One of the two female voices is Ingrid Oppermann's. She had started studying at DFFB in 1970. Quite likely, the film school provided the infrastructure to make this film with little means, using the optical printer and other facilities. Moreover, the script or scenario reproduced in this booklet was found in Skip Norman's DFFB file.

Finally, it is worth noting that the production history of *On Africa* also features East Berlin. As the director of photography Resa Dabui recalls, Dabui and Skip Norman boarded their flight to West Africa in the Eastern part of the city. They took the plane to Luanda, Angola. One of the photographs included in the film shows the two of them at the airport. Once they had gotten there, they were stuck at the airport without a shooting permit. At this point, *On Africa* risked failing altogether as a film project. It seems to have been rescued at the editing table at DFFB.

Volker Pantenburg

Hidden Persuader

Almost halfway into *On Africa*, for the first (yet, not the last) time, the voice-over utters the term "neo-colonialism." An initial attempt at a definition conveys some of its conceptual contours: "Neo-colonialism is the control of formally independent states by groups of big financial capital. These groups are supported by imperialist governments."[1]

These words are delivered over (or alongside) a percussive soundtrack and the sight of (briefly flickering) photographs of a Texaco gas station and four snapshots of nondescript vernacular buildings, all presumably taken out of the window of a car driving through the outskirts of Luanda. Bookending the photographs is the first of altogether five intertitles spelling "NEO-COLONIALISM" in capital letters.

For approximately five minutes that follow, the voice-over elaborates on the subject, alternately accompanied by drums and other noises (some of which resemble those of a cash register) as well as more drive-by photographs of street scenes, supplemented by sequences of lists and diagrams of transnational financial networks, the former presented on a background of the national flags of the United Kingdom, France, and West Germany.

Importantly, however, by introducing the term "neo-colonialism," the film also introduces one of its main protagonists (albeit without providing a name or making direct reference to his writings). Apparently, Joey Gibbs and Skip Norman did not consider it necessary to disclose the main source of their concepts, statistical data, and *verbatim* formulations.

For this section of the film is based on Kwame Nkrumah's 1965 book *Neo-Colonialism: The Last Stage of Imperialism*. Nkrumah, the first prime minister and president of independent Ghana, as well as an anticolonial intellectual and politician *par*

---

1 Translated from the German text as read by Klaus Wildenhahn.

excellence, developed and communicated his Pan-Africanist (and increasingly socialist) politics by way of a series of compendious treatises.

Credited with having provided the most comprehensive conceptual elaboration of neocolonialism and having firmly supplanted it into the critical discourse of the anti-imperialist and anti-capitalist African left, the lines probably most quoted from his book (yet omitted by Gibbs and Norman) are the following: "The essence of neo-colonialism is that the State which is subject to it is, in theory, independent and has all the outward trappings of international sovereignty. In reality its economic system and thus its political policy is directed from outside."[2]

Though the controversial Nkrumah was widely considered to be its main author, whether he actually wrote this book (and others) himself remains a somewhat disputed fact, not least in the eyes of the very forces of imperialism that he called out in the subtitle. After a longer period in the 1950s and early '60s during which Ghana had been a close economic partner and political ally of the United States, under the impression of the killing of his Congolese equal Patrice Lumumba in 1961, a crime that had at least in part been pushed and commissioned by the CIA, Nkrumah began to rethink his relationship with the US, which he considered to be the most powerful proponent of "neo-colonialism," a shadowy type of rule, which he believed was even more pernicious than traditional colonialism.

When the book was published in 1965, the American officials were furious. Washington viewed Nkrumah's attacks with profound concern, disturbed by the book's "deeply disturbing and offensive" anti-American tone. On February 24, 1966, three months after the United States had voiced their indignation, Nkrumah was overthrown in a military *coup d'état* and was forced to seek exile in Guinea, where he stayed until his death in 1972.

Thus, Gibbs and Norman paid—more or less hidden—homage to a socialist leader and his theory of neocolonial exploitation and dependency.[3] Further direct quotations from Nkrumah's book relate to monetary politics, the "use of high rates of interest" as "another technique of neo-colonialism,"[4] and the balkanization of Africa by the maintenance of the "seven major currency groups."[5]

Apart from some who may have been aware of the accusations by the East German authorities, voiced repeatedly against West Germany's "Neo-Kolonialismus" (allegedly taking advantage, economically and strategically, of the worsened reputation of greater colonial powers such as the UK or France in Africa), a West German audience lacked fluency in the concept of neocolonialism. Nkrumah's 1965 book has never been translated into German (other than previous titles such as *Consciencism; Africa Must Unite;* or his autobiography, titled *Ghana*). And in the same year, 1965, in an article on the "European Periphery," Hans Magnus Enzensberger maintained: "What the poor world says is [...] hardly taken note of. Its spokesmen and theorists are hardly translated, still less read. Kwame Nkrumah is considered a dull shouter, Fidel Castro a bearded windbag, Frantz Fanon, whose writings exert an enormous influence on the African and Asian intelligentsia, is an unknown quantity among us."[6]

Four, five years on, interest in Third World intellectuals such as Fanon or Nkrumah might have increased among anti-imperialist

---

2 Kwame Nkrumah, *Neo-Colonialism: The Last Stage of Imperialism,* New York, 1965, ix.

3 The sentence quoted earlier from *On Africa* in all likelihood derived from this passage of Nkrumah's book: "modern neo-colonialism is based upon the control of nominally independent States by giant financial interests. These interests often act through or on behalf of a particular capitalist State, but they are quite capable of acting on their own and forcing those imperial countries in which they have a dominant interest to follow their lead." See ibid., 22.

4 Ibid., 241.

5 Ibid., 220.

6 Hans Magnus Enzensberger, "Europäische Peripherie," *Kursbuch 2,* (August 1965), 154–73, here: 164.

circles in West Berlin or Frankfurt. However, even around 1970, Nkrumah was far from being a household name for the larger West German public. Much less his decolonial political economy, which Gibbs and Norman volleyed onto the TV screen with astonishing determination, to be swallowed by a one-off prime-time audience, which may or may not have taken notes.

Tom Holert

Paratexts / (Retroactive) Scripts
Or
"The last letter from Patrice Lumumba to his wife answers all skeptical questions."

Apart from an extensive file and retroactive script concerning his film *Blues People* (1968), three concepts that Skip Norman wrote alongside his film projects can be found in the DFFB student files in the Schriftgutarchiv at Deutsche Kinemathek, Berlin: his presumably very first draft for a film called "Max" (which was never realized), the proposal for his diploma film *Strange Fruit* (1969), and one for the film *On Africa* (1970), which he produced in collaboration with Joey Gibbs.

The film "Max," according to the proposal, was planned as a short feature to be filmed on ORWO Super 8. The file consists of a fourteen-line concept, the complete "production announcement," and several location sketches to indicate the positions of the camera and actors. The plot is about two men who meet in Copenhagen, one of them African, the other an African American: "One is confident, the other insecure." The relationship between the two men is complicated and problematic: "One treats the other with contempt, only in the jazz club do they come closer through music. The culture connection is not able to maintain the human connection." The encounter ends in murder. In a letter from December 1966, Skip Norman's tutor at the time, filmmaker and DFFB codirector Erwin Leiser, stipulated that Norman should continue his studies and gain more experience before making this film.

The second concept is for Norman's diploma film *Strange Fruit*. On two typewritten pages, he develops a reflection on what it means to live as an expatriate in Europe while the Civil Rights Movement is taking place in the United States. I quote a longer passage from this impressive document, which was written in German:

"Since World War II, there has existed in Europe a group of African Americans and other people of color who, for various reasons, mostly psycho-political, turned their backs on their homeland. Because the social climate in Europe was very open, they quickly found their way and did not feel the tremendous pressure of inferiority (at least not at first) ... .

"Veterans (freedom fighters on European soil) stayed behind and those who could afford the expensive journey, inspired by the hopelessness of the struggle for equality, emigrated. Numerically there were not many of them, but enough to make their presence felt in their new territory over time. As Europe began to react allergically to its expatriates, the struggle for equal rights, driven by students in southern colleges and universities, became more spirited.

"... No more being patient, working themselves to death and praying, but freedom NOW. The Civil Rights Act came into force in 1964.

"While the expatriate was losing more and more his psychological footing in his new situation, his brothers at home had come a long way, psychologically of course. Economic conditions in Europe were still more favorable."

Skip Norman ends his short essay-as-scenario with the question: "What role do expatriates play within the global political constellation? Is expatriatism justified today?" The film was broadcast on Westdeutscher Rundfunk (WDR) on August 7, 1971.

The third concept is the description of *On Africa* published in this booklet. It must have been written in the postproduction phase. Joey Gibbs, Skip Norman's collaborator for the scenario, had just returned from Moscow and was (according to cinematographer Resa Dabui's recollection) "the pseudo-political head" of the production.

The text is almost identical to that of the film with a few exceptions and some information given on the side that mentions formal or strategic elements: "Tracking shot passing pedestrians (negative effect); Photomontage of Portuguese prosperity compared to Angola (didactics) ... ."

In the introduction, Norman and Gibbs write: "Through a dynamic combination of film technique and partisan sensibility in dealing with the facts, it shows the strength and weakness of Europe as a result of the colonial age: the weakness and strength of Africa as proof of Africa's rebirth." (To express partisanship, the German tapeworm word "Partisanenempfindungsvermögen" / "a capacity to hold partisan sentiments" is used.)

I see these concepts as paratexts, two of them written as a means of communicating the starting point and justification for a filmic work within the learning environment of the Berlin film school DFFB where Skip Norman was part of the first year after its inauguration. I read the first two concepts as reflections on certain issues that defined Skip Norman's position in the early 1970s. The third one seems to be a necessary production outline, presumably for WDR—which was much less bureaucratic then than it is now. It is worth noting that *On Africa* was broadcast by WDR at nine in the evening of Saturday, May 20, 1972.

A postscript, from the practical point of view: According to the cinematographer Resa Dabui their team didn't get permission to shoot once they had arrived in Angola at Luanda airport. One of the photos in the film shows the two of them sitting at a table in the airport. All they could do was take a taxi and secretly shoot some photos from the car. I find these ephemeral photos, wrested from the circumstances of the shooting ban, striking and touching in their casualness. And I also see a strong statement in using them in this particular way—as enhancement of the much more "austere" neocolonial construct of the film. After their return, Norman worked with Resa Dabui and the latter's small Pathé Baby camera, equipped to expose single frames manually, and—supported by co-student and cinematographer Carlos Bustamante—with the optical printer that Helmut Herbst had installed at the DFFB.

Madeleine Bernstorff

Patterns of Improvisation

Scaling, vertical order. *On Africa* is made with limited technical resources and very little footage while its issue *on Africa*—a huge imagery at a particularly violent phase in the history of the African continent and its decolonial struggles for independence—is spotted from a highly loaded place, that is, Berlin.

It is 1969, Angola is at war. The film takes shape, but the permission to shoot in Angola is denied. So where to get footage, how to address the missing image? How to turn the longing for an image into a cinematic option? Why not go elsewhere?

Instead of making a retreat or giving in to defeat, the filmmakers insist on going on, finding footage, and, back in Berlin, editing it. *On Africa* becomes a test in operating the difference between what they hope to do and what they finally have at hand; a method that sets in motion images and sounds from a personal collection of images found in books, magazines, and photos gathered in Germany and juxtaposed with the small amount of footage taken in and around the airport of Luanda. What is there is poor, but not necessarily limited. The experience leads to a film about the transition from a concept of what the film should have been to what it can be. It is a piece of improvisation. It demonstrates a method of combining and juxtaposing, of collaging and remixing scant material, evoking a vast cine-geography, picturing a multi-continental issue with almost nothing.

Improvisation, horizontal order. We can learn from jazz music that improvisation goes along with repetition and difference. Difference in repetition is what is happening in *On Africa*. A rhythm develops out of a montage of images, material in negative of traveling shots in Berlin, black film leader alternating with images of historical figures and places found in printed matter, drive-by takes in Luanda contrasting with maps, diagrams, and animations generated at the optical printer (with the help of Helmut Herbst) and takes of Black people at work. Repetitive patterns, the reuse of the same footage, make improvisation visible and audible in all kinds of sounds, music, and spoken words. Some titles and tracks relate to Skip Norman's previous films made in Berlin. *Blues People* (1968) alludes to the book of the same title by LeRoi Jones (1963); in *On Africa*, we can listen again to the drum and percussion pieces by Billy Brook used in Norman's *Strange Fruit* (DFFB graduate film, 1969). Skip Norman collaborates with some Berlin-based African American musicians, Brook and Donald Coleman among others. "Strange Fruit," the poem by Abel Meeropol, sung by Billie Holliday, in Norman's Germany-based filmmaking, significantly connects the experience of the physical violence against Black people in the US with the violence and struggle for liberation on the African continent and in juxtaposition with Berlin, the place of colonial division 1884. *On Africa* is obviously the junction of numerous traces and matters triangulating Berlin, the US, and the continent.

Overexposure, underexposure. Comes into play with another layer of improvisation, the voice-over text written by Skip Norman and Joey Gibbs and spoken by DFFB acquaintances Ingrid Oppermann (a friend of Skip Norman and actor in *Inextinguishable Fire* and other films by Harun Farocki), Li Antes (who plays in *Blues People*), and Klaus Wildenhahn (TV documentary filmmaker and DFFB teacher at the time).

As the German voice states, "Afrika" is divided in climatic zones, the continent again is cut into areas (alluding to the logic of area studies and patterns of commodification), humidity, heat, vegetation, rainfall. The voices take over in their German pronunciation of "Afrika." "Afrika hat," "Afrika ist," "Afrika charakterisiert": quotes, reuses of overgeneralizing language. But the German voicing, inadvertently, is tilting toward the voice-of-god authority if not condescension. The text doesn't ask, it declares and explains. It could have been a mocking rip-off, an ironical comment, a provocation, echoing the colonial logic in documentary traditions, the rhetoric of "underdevelopment," the continuities in racified prejudices towards African contexts in the German perspective, if the speakers had played with, or mimicked, these accents or accentuations. The most discomforting part of the film is indeed the German voice-over, the text, the voicing, as signifiers of power play. It is not clear to me where the reproduction of the violence it exposes leads to. The film intentionally or unintentionally points at the fact that colonialism affects German language, too. What, then, does repetition do to words and numbers? How can this heritage be debunked? What would have happened had Skip Norman lent his voice to the German text?

On Africa is full of contradictory echoes. It is also resonant of previous experimental films made in Berlin in the context of DFFB, which tested out militancy, the power of speech in combination with different landscapes of the visual. By the end, the text addresses the militant liberation movements, and sounds of guns take over. Sounds of gunshots give rhythm to the flickering images. Rhythm, the shooting, the anger resonates from *Strange Fruit* in which Bobby Seale explains "the power of the gun" as being a tool of restitution of rights. The rhythm of gunshots finally leads to the heartbeat, another repeated beat, in time with images of Patrice Lumumba, guiding the film towards a new physical and narrative direction.

Following the traces laid by *On Africa*, the question of improvisation finally extends to us: what do we spectators today bring to the fore, what do we see and what do we hear in *On Africa*, and what do we bear in mind?

Marie-Hélène Gutberlet

Editorial Note

The document published in this issue was found in the personal file of Wilbert Reuben Norman, Jr., known as Skip, in the Schriftgutarchiv of the Deutsche Film- und Fernsehakademie Berlin (DFFB). The text largely corresponds to the voice-over commentary of *On Africa*, a film Skip Norman completed in 1970, after graduating with a degree in directing. He cowrote the screenplay with Joey Gibbs and shared the camera work with Resa Dabui and Carlos Bustamante. We can assume that the film was self-produced since the mailing address of the Denso Film production company is Skip Norman's home address at the time. The document from the archives only has the text; for the present publication, we have followed the detailed indications of which images were to accompany the spoken text and have added them on the opposite pages. Patrice Lumumba's letter to his wife, featured in the "Material" section, is not part of the document in the DFFB file. In the film, accompanied by a steady thumping percussive noise that sounds like the beating of a heart, it is printed as scrolling text for more than four minutes at the end of the film.

Skip Norman, born in Baltimore in 1933, had left the US in the early 1960s to study German, theater, and medicine in Göttingen. In 1966, he moved to Berlin to join the newly founded DFFB. By 1969, he had made the films *Riffi* (1966), *Blues People* (1968), *Cultural Nationalism* (1969), and the graduation film *Strange Fruit* (1969). Norman collaborated on many films by other students as a cinematographer or actor, including Harun Farocki's *Their Newspapers* and *White Christmas* (both 1968), *Break the Power of the Manipulators* (1968) by Helke Sander, and *The 4 Gestures* (1969) by Wolf Gremm. After graduating from the DFFB, Norman continued to be involved in many films by former fellow students, such as Jonatan Briel. Returning to the US in the mid-1970s, Norman began studying for a bachelor's degree, earning a masters and eventually a doctorate in Visual Anthropology. His work as a photographer and ethnographer eventually led him to Northern Cyprus, where he taught as a professor of Visual Ethnography from the beginning of 1996 at Eastern Mediterranean University in Famagusta. He died in 2015 in Washington, DC.

On Africa was screened on October 7, 1970 at the XIX. Internationale Filmwoche Mannheim (IFFM) in the section "Informationsschau" ("Information Show"). In the festival's program booklet, arranged alphabetically, the film is sandwiched between the DFFB production *Omnia vincit amor* ("Love Conquers All," 1970) by Norman's friend and colleague Georg Lehner, and *Wind from the East* by Groupe Dziga Vertov, here attributed to Jean-Luc Godard. We do not know about other festival or theatrical screenings of Skip Norman's film.

Westdeutscher Rundfunk (WDR) (commissioning editor: Georg Alexander) broadcast *On Africa* on Saturday, May 20, 1972, together with *Bloody River* (1970) by Richard Besrodinoff and *Die industrielle Reservearmee* (1971) by Helma Sanders in the program "Political Short Films from the FRG." The fact that a program such as this could be shown on television at nine on a Saturday evening says a lot about the possibilities and leeway of the public broadcasters at that time.

The only 16-mm print of the film known to us was found in the archives of the WDR. It was digitized by the Harun Farocki Institut in 2021. After the premiere of the digitized version at the "Archival Assembly #1" festival in September 2021, the film was presented together with Farocki's *Their Newspapers* at the "Visible Evidence" conference in Frankfurt am Main in December of the same year. The texts published here are based on the brief comments presented there by Madeleine Bernstorff, Marie-Hélène Gutberlet, Tom Holert, and Volker Pantenburg. Sónia Vaz Borges was unable to participate due to illness. We are pleased that she was able to write her commentary for the issue.

Volker Pantenburg, for the Harun Farocki Institut, July 2023

Imprint

Editor: Volker Pantenburg
Managing Editor: Elsa de Seynes
Proofreading: Mandi Gomez
Design: Daniela Burger, buerodb.de; Assistance: Alix Stria
Lithography: prints-professional, Berlin

Printing: Druckhaus Sportflieger, Berlin
Fonts: Neutral BP, Excelsior
Paper: Munken Lynx, Efalin Feinleinen
Print Run: 1500
ISBN: 978-2-940672-50-9

Thanks to Antje Ehmann, Anna Faroqhi, Lara Faroqhi
as well as Skip Norman's family, and Thomas Büchel, Carlos Bustamante, Kodwo Eshun, Brigitta Kuster, Pascal Maslon, Laliv Melamed, Doreen Mende, Markus Ruff, Alexandra Symons Sutcliffe, Stefanie Schulte Strathaus, Sara Stevenson

© 2023, the authors and the Harun Farocki Institut, Berlin
Published by the Harun Farocki Institut with Motto Books

More information on Skip Norman and his work:

www.harun-farocki-institut.org
HaFI 018

HaFI 018 was realized in cooperation with the German Film Office, an initiative of German Films and the Goethe-Institut, and with financial support from the Department of Film Studies at the University of Zurich.

Impressum

Herausgeber: Volker Pantenburg
Redaktion: Elsa de Seynes
Gestaltung: Daniela Burger, buerodb.de; Assistenz: Alix Stria
Lithografie: prints-professional, Berlin

Druck: Druckhaus Sportflieger, Berlin
Fonts: Neutral BP, Excelsior
Papier: Munken Lynx, Efalin Feinleinen
Auflage: 1500
ISBN: 978-2-940672-50-9

Dank an: Antje Ehmann, Anna Faroqhi, Lara Faroqhi
sowie Skip Normans Familie und Thomas Büchel, Carlos Bustamante, Kodwo Eshun, Brigitta
Kuster, Pascal Maslon, Laliv Melamed, Doreen Mende, Markus Ruff, Alexandra Symons
Sutcliffe, Stefanie Schulte Strathaus, Sara Stevenson

© 2023, die Autor*innen und Harun Farocki Institut, Berlin
Veröffentlicht von Harun Farocki Institut mit Motto Books

Mehr Informationen zu Skip Norman und seinem Werk:

www.harun-farocki-institut.org
HaFI 018

HaFI 018 wurde in Kooperation mit dem German Film Office, einer Initiative von German Films
und dem Goethe-Institut und mit Mitteln des Seminars für Filmwissenschaft der Universität
Zürich produziert.

Editorische Notiz

Das in diesem Heft abgedruckte Dokument stammt aus der Personenakte von Wilbert Reuben Norman, Jr., genannt Skip, im Schriftgutarchiv der Deutschen Kinemathek. Der Text entspricht weitgehend dem Voice-over-Kommentar von *On Africa,* einem Film, den Skip Norman im Jahr 1970, nach dem Abschluss seines Regiestudiums, fertigstellte. Das Drehbuch schrieb er mit Joey Gibbs, die Kameraarbeit teilte er sich mit Resa Dabui. Der Film ist eine Eigenproduktion, darauf deutet die Postadresse der Denso Film-Produktion hin, die mit Skip Normans Privatadresse zu diesem Zeitpunkt übereinstimmt. Das Archivdokument besteht nur aus dem Text; für die vorliegende Veröffentlichung sind wir den Angaben gefolgt, welche Bilder der gesprochene Text jeweils begleiten sollte, und haben sie auf den gegenüberliegenden Seiten hinzugefügt. Der Brief Patrice Lumumbas an seine Frau ist nicht Teil des Dokuments in der DFFB-Akte. Im Film ist er, begleitet von einem perkussiven Geräusch, das wie das Schlagen eines Herzens klingt, am Ende des Films mehr als vier Minuten lang als Rolltext zu lesen.

Skip Norman, 1933 in Baltimore geboren, hatte die USA zu Beginn der 1960er-Jahre verlassen, um in Göttingen Deutsch, Theaterwissenschaft und Medizin zu studieren. 1966 zog er nach Berlin, um an die neugegründete DFFB zu wechseln. Bis 1969 entstanden die Filme *Riffi* (1966), *Blues People* (1968), *Cultural Nationalism* (1969) und der Abschlussfilm *Strange Fruit* (1969). Norman arbeitete an vielen Filmen anderer Student*innen als Kameramann oder Darsteller mit, unter anderem an Harun Farockis *Ihre Zeitungen* und *White Christmas* (beide 1968), *Brecht die Macht der Manipulateure* (1968) von Helke Sander oder *Die 4 Gesten* (1969) von Wolf Gremm. Auch nach seinem Abschluss an der DFFB war er an vielen Filmen von ehemaligen Kommilitonen, etwa Jonatan Briel, beteiligt. Mitte der 1970er-Jahre kehrte Norman zurück in die USA, begann ein BA-Studium, machte einen MA-

und schließlich eine PhD-Abschluss in Visueller Anthropologie. Die Arbeit als Fotograf und Ethnograf führte ihn schließlich nach Nord-Zypern, wo er ab 1996 als Professor für Visuelle Ethnographie an der Eastern Mediterranean University in Famagusta lehrte. Er starb 2015 in Washington, DC.

On Africa wurde am 7. Oktober 1970 bei der XIX. Internationalen Filmwoche Mannheim in der „Informationsschau" aufgeführt; im alphabetischen Programmheft des Festivals steht der Film zwischen der DFFB-Produktion *Omnia vincit amor* (1970) von Normans Freund und Kollegen Georg Lehner sowie *Ostwind* des Groupe Dziga Vertov, der kurzerhand Jean-Luc Godard zugeschrieben wird. Über weitere Festival- oder Kinovorführungen ist zum jetzigen Zeitpunkt nichts bekannt.

Der WDR (Redaktion: Georg Alexander) strahlte *On Africa* am Samstag, 20. Mai 1972 gemeinsam mit *Bloody River* (1970) von Richard Besrodinoff und *Die industrielle Reservearmee* (1971) von Helma Sanders im Programm „Politische Kurzfilme aus der BRD" aus. Dass ein solches Programm an einem Samstagabend um 21 Uhr im Fernsehen gezeigt werden konnte, sagt viel über die Möglichkeiten und Spielräume der öffentlich-rechtlichen Sender in dieser Zeit. Im Archiv des WDR fand sich die einzige uns bekannte 16mm-Kopie des Films, die 2021 vom Harun Farocki Institut digitalisiert wurde. Nach der Wiederaufführung beim Festival „Archival Assembly #1" wurde der Film im Dezember 2021 gemeinsam mit Farockis *Ihre Zeitungen* bei der Konferenz „Visible Evidence" in Frankfurt am Main vorgestellt. Auf den dort vorgetragenen Kurzkommentaren von Madeleine Bernstorff, Marie-Hélène Gutberlet, Tom Holert und Volker Pantenburg basieren die hier abgedruckten Kurztexte. Sónia Vaz Borges konnte krankheitsbedingt nicht teilnehmen. Wir freuen uns, dass sie ihren Kommentar für das Heft schreiben konnte.

Volker Pantenburg, für das Harun Farocki Institut, Juli 2023

zu *Blues People* (1968). In *On Africa* kann man Schlagzeug- und Perkussion-Stücke von Billy Brook hören, wie zuvor in Normans DFFB Abschlussfilm *Strange Fruit* (1969). Skip Norman arbeitet mit einigen in Berlin lebenden African-American Musikern, darunter Brook und Donald Coleman. „Strange Fruit", das Gedicht von Abel Meeropol, das Billie Holliday singt, verbindet in Normans Filmemachen in Deutschland die Erfahrung physischer Gewalt gegen Schwarze Menschen in den USA mit der Gewalt und dem Befreiungskampf auf dem Afrikanischen Kontinent in Verbindung zu Berlin, dem Ort der kolonialen Teilung in 1884. *On Africa* offenbart die Kreuzung solcher Spuren im Dreieck Berlin, USA und dem Kontinent.

Überbelichtung, Unterbelichtung. Auf einer weiteren Improvisationsebene kommt der Voice-over Text zum Tragen, den Skip Norman und Joey Gibbs schreiben und DFFB-Bekannte Ingrid Oppermann (eine Freundin von Skip Norman und Darstellerin in *Nicht löschbares Feuer* und anderen Filmen von Harun Farocki), Li Antes (sie spielt auch in *Blues People*) und Klaus Wildenhahn (Dokumentarfilmemacher beim NDR und zu diesem Zeitpunkt Lehrer an der DFFB) einsprechen.

Dann sagen die deutschen Stimmen „Afrika", und der Kontinent wird wieder in Klimazonen segmentiert (ganz den Area Studies und ihren Verwertungsmustern folgend), Feuchtigkeit, Hitze, Vegetation, Regen. Die deutschen Stimmen übernehmen „Afrika". „Afrika hat". „Afrika ist". „Afrika charakterisiert", zitieren, wiederholen verallgemeinernde Sprache. Unversehens kippt das deutsche Sprechen in die Voice-of-god Autorität, zuweilen despektierlich. Der Text fragt nicht, er deklariert, erklärt. Er hätte höhnischer Schlagabtausch, ironischer Kommentar, Provokation, Echo der kolonialen Verfasstheit in der Geschichte des Dokumentarfilms, auf die „Unterentwicklungs"-Rhetorik, auf die Kontinuitäten rassifizierter Vorurteile gegenüber Afrikanischen Kontexten werden können, wenn die Sprechenden Akzente oder Akzentuierungen nachgeahmt, überzogen oder mit ihnen gespielt hätten. Der unangenehmste Teil des Films ist in der Tat das deutschsprachige Voice-over, Signifikant des Machtspiels. Mir ist nicht klar, wohin die Reproduktion dieser Gewalt führt. Der Film weist absichtlich oder unabsichtlich auf die Tatsache hin, dass Kolonialismus auch die deutsche Sprache durchtränkt. Was machen Wiederholungen hier mit Worten und Zahlen? Wie kann dieses Erbe entmachtet werden? Was wäre, wenn Skip Norman selbst den deutschen Text eingesprochen hätte?

In *On Africa* hallen viele Widersprüche wider. Auch vorherige Filmexperimente im Umfeld der DFFB, in denen Militanz, die Macht des Wortes in Verbindung zu verschiedenen visuellen Landschaften ausgetestet wurden. Zum Ende spricht der Text bewaffnete Befreiungsbewegungen an, dann übernehmen Schüsse die Tonspur. Die Schussgeräusche geben den flackernden Bildern einen Rhythmus. Die Wut aus *Strange Fruit* hallt nach, wo Bobby Seal „the power of the gun" als Mittel der Restitution erklärt. Die Schüsse gehen schließlich in einen Herzschlag über, auch das ein Beat, der kurz mit Bildern von Patrice Lumumba zusammengeführt wird und den Film in eine neue körperliche und narrative Richtung lenkt.

Folgt man den Spuren in *On Africa,* erreicht die Frage der Improvisation zuletzt uns: was bringen wir Zuschauer*innen heute ein, was sehen wir und was hören wir in *On Africa,* und welche Auseinandersetzung löst all das aus?

Marie-Hélène Gutberlet

dungsvermögen in der Bearbeitung der Fakten [zeigt der Film] die Stärke und Schwäche Europas als Folge des Kolonialalters: die Schwäche und Stärke Afrikas als Beweis für die Wiedergeburt Afrikas."

Die Konzepte sind Paratexte, geschrieben, um Ausgangspunkt und Rechtfertigung für die filmische Arbeit innerhalb der Lern-umgebung der Filmschule zu vermitteln, an der Skip Norman im ersten Jahr nach ihrer Eröffnung studierte. Ich lese sie als Refle-xionen zu Themen, die Skip Norman in den frühen 1970er-Jahren beschäftigten. Der dritte Text erscheint als notwendiges Produktions-Skript, vermutlich für den Sender WDR. Erwähnenswert ist, dass On Africa 1972 an einem Samstagabend um 21 Uhr gesendet wurde.

Postskriptum aus der Praxis: Das kleine Team erhielt laut Kameramann Resa Dabui nach der Ankunft am Flughafen in Angola keine Drehgenehmigung. Es blieb ihnen nichts anderes übrig, als ein Taxi zu nehmen und heimlich ein paar Fotos aus dem Auto heraus zu schießen. Diese flüchtigen Fotos, den Umständen des Drehverbots abgerungen, wirken in ihrer Beiläufigkeit beeindruckend und berührend. Ich sehe eine starke Aussage darin, sie auf diese besondere Weise zu ver-wenden – als Bereicherung des viel „stren-geren" neokolonialen Konstrukts des Films. Nach der Rückkehr arbeitete Norman mit Resa Dabui und dessen kleiner Pathé-Baby-Kamera, mit der die manuelle Belichtung von Einzelbildern möglich war, und – unter-stützt vom Kommilitonen und Kameramann Carlos Bustamante – an dem Tricktisch, den Helmut Herbst an der DFFB installiert hatte.

Madeleine Bernstorff

Improvisationsmuster

Maßstab, vertikale Ordnung. On Africa entsteht mit sehr begrenzten technischen Mitteln und Filmmaterial, während Afrika, diese gigan-tische Vorstellungsfläche des afrikanischen Kontinents in der gewalttätigen historischen Phase seiner Dekolonisierung, von Berlin aus auf den Plan gerufen wird.

1969, in Angola ist Krieg. On Africa nimmt Formen an, aber die Drehgenehmigung für Angola wird abgelehnt. Wo Bilder hernehmen, wie ihr Fehlen adressieren? Wie den Bilder-Wunsch in eine filmische Geste verwandeln? Warum unbedingt Angola?

Die Filmemacher bestehen darauf weiterzu-machen, hinzufliegen, Footage zu finden, das sie später in Berlin schneiden. On Africa: ein Test im Umgang mit der Differenz zwischen dem Erhofften und dem, was sie schließlich zur Hand haben. Eine Form ent-steht, die in Deutschland gesammelte Bilder und Töne in Bewegung versetzt und mit dem Footage aus und um den Flughafen von Luanda konfrontiert. Was sie haben, ist arm, aber deshalb nicht begrenzt. Die Erfahrung führt zu einem Film, einem Improvisations-stück. Er demonstriert eine Methode des Kombinierens und Gegenüberstellens, des Collagierens und Remixens, das so eine multi-kontinentale Cine-Geografie entwirft.

Improvisation, horizontale Ordnung. Jazz-musik lehrt uns, dass Improvisation mit Wiederholung und Differenz einhergeht. Dif-ferenz und Wiederholung machen On Africa aus. Aus der Montage der Bilder entwickelt sich ein Rhythmus aus dem abwechselnd montierten Negativmaterial von Kamerafahrten durch Berlin, Schwarzfilm und gefundenen Bildern historischer Figuren und Orte, Fahrten in Luanda, Landkarten, Diagrammen und Animationen, die (mit der Hilfe von Helmut Herbst) am Tricktisch entstehen.

Wiederholungen, die Wiederverwendung desselben Materials, machen Improvisation sichtbar und auch in allerlei Sounds, Musik, gesprochener Sprache hörbar. Manche der Tracks nehmen Fäden zu Skip Normans vorherigen Berliner Filmen auf, zum Beispiel

Paratexte / (nachträgliche) Skripte
oder
„Der letzte Brief Patrice Lumumbas an seine
Frau beantwortet alle skeptischen Fragen."

Neben umfangreichem Material sowie einem
nachträglichen Drehbuch zu Skip Normans
Film *Blues People* (1968) finden sich in den
DFFB-Akten im Schriftgutarchiv der Deutschen Kinemathek drei Konzepte für Film-
projekte: Normans vermutlich allererster
Entwurf für den Film „Max", (nicht realisiert),
sowie die Skripte für den Diplomfilm *Strange
Fruit* (1969) und *On Africa* (1970).

Der Film „Max" war als Kurzspielfilm auf
ORWO Super 8 geplant. Im Dossier finden
sich das 14-zeilige Konzept, die vollständige
Produktionsankündigung sowie mehrere
Skizzen der Drehorte mit Positionen für Kamera und Schauspieler. Zwei Männer treffen
sich in Kopenhagen, einer von ihnen Afrikaner, der andere Afroamerikaner. „Der eine
ist selbstbewusst, der andere unsicher." Die
Beziehung zwischen den beiden Männern
ist kompliziert und problematisch. „Der eine
behandelt den anderen mit Verachtung,
nur im Jazzclub kommen sie sich über die
Musik näher. Die kulturelle Verbindung
ist nicht in der Lage, die menschliche Verbindung aufrechtzuerhalten." Die Begegnung
sollte mit einem Mord enden. In einem Brief
vom Dezember 1966 rät Normans Tutor, der
Filmemacher und DFFB-Ko-Direktor Erwin
Leiser, dem Filmstudenten das Studium fortzusetzen und erst einmal mehr Erfahrung
zu sammeln.

Das zweite Konzept ist für Normans Diplomfilm *Strange Fruit*. Auf zwei Schreibmaschin-
enseiten entwickelt er eine Reflexion
darüber, was es bedeutet, als *expatriate* in
Europa zu leben, während der Bürgerrechts-
bewegung in den USA. Hier eine längere
Passage aus diesem beeindruckenden,
deutschsprachigen Dokument:

„Seit dem Zweiten Weltkrieg existiert in
Europa eine Gruppe von Afroamerikanern
und anderen Persons of Color [Farbigen], die
aus verschiedenen Gründen, meist psycho-
politischer Natur ihre Rücken der Heimat zu-

gekehrt haben. Weil das Sozialklima Europas
sehr aufgeschlossen war, fanden sie sich
schnell zurecht und spürten nicht den unge-
heuren Druck der Minderwertigkeit (auf
jeden Fall vorläufig nicht) … Veteranen (Frei-
heitskämpfer auf europäischem Boden)
blieben zurück, und die, die die teure Reise
bezahlen konnten, von der Aussichtslosigkeit
des Gleichberechtigungskampfes angeregt,
wanderten aus. Zahlenmäßig waren es nicht
viele, aber genug, um sich mit der Zeit in
ihrem neuen Territorium bemerkbar zu machen. Als Europa auf seine Expatrioten
allergisch zu reagieren begann, wurde der
Kampf in den Staaten um die Gleichberech-
tigung, von den Studenten in den Colleges
und Universitäten des Südens angetrieben,
lebhafter. … Nicht mehr sich gedulden, sich
totarbeiten und beten, sondern Freiheit NOW.
Das Bürgerrechtsgesetz trat 1964 in Kraft.
Während der Expatriot in seiner neuen Situation mehr und mehr psychologischen
Halt verlor, waren seine Brüder daheim we-
sentlich weiter gekommen, psychologisch,
natürlich. Die economischen Bedingungen
in Europa waren immer noch günstiger."

Skip Norman endet mit der Frage: „Welche
Rolle spielen die Expatrioten in der welt-
politischen Constellation? Ist Expatriotismus
heute gerechtfertigt?"
Der Film wurde am 7. August 1971 um 21 Uhr
im WDR ausgestrahlt.

Das dritte Konzept ist die in diesem Heft
abgedruckte Beschreibung von *On Africa,*
geschrieben in der Postproduktionsphase.
Joey Gibbs, Skip Normans Mitarbeiter am
Drehbuch, war gerade erst aus Moskau zu-
rückgekehrt. Laut Kameramann Resa Dabui
war Gibbs *„der pseudopolitische Kopf"* der
Produktion.

Der Text ist fast identisch mit dem Film-
text, mit wenigen zusätzlichen Hinweisen auf
formale oder strategische Mittel: „Fahrt an
Fußgängern vorbei (Negativeffekt); Fotomontage portugiesischer Wohlstand Angola
gegenüber (Didaktik) …"

In der Einleitung schreiben Norman und
Gibbs: „… durch eine dynamische Kombination
von Filmtechnik und Partisanenempfin-

wurde Nkrumah durch einen Militärputsch gestürzt und gezwungen, ins Exil nach Guinea zu gehen, wo er bis zu seinem Tod 1972 blieb.

Auf ihre Weise zollten Gibbs und Norman – mehr oder weniger versteckt – einem sozialistischen Führer und seiner Theorie der neokolonialen Ausbeutung und Abhängigkeit Tribut.[2] Weitere direkte Zitate aus Nkrumahs Buch beziehen sich auf die Währungspolitik, die „Benutzung hoher Zinssätze" als „eine andere Methode des Neo-Kolonialismus"[3] sowie die Balkanisierung Afrikas durch die Beibehaltung der „sieben Hauptwährungsgruppen in Afrika".[4]

Abgesehen von einigen, die vielleicht die wiederholt geäußerten Vorwürfe der DDR-Propaganda gegen den „Neo-Kolonialismus" der Bundesrepublik kannten (der angeblich den wirtschaftlich und strategisch schlechten Ruf größerer Kolonialmächte wie des Vereinigten Königreichs oder Frankreichs in Afrika ausnutzte), war das westdeutsche Publikum mit dem Konzept des Neokolonialismus eher nicht vertraut. Nkrumahs Buch ist nie ins Deutsche übersetzt worden (anders als frühere Titel wie *Consciencism; Africa Must Unite;* oder seine Autobiographie mit dem Titel *Ghana*). Und im Jahr seines Erscheinens, 1965, stellte Hans Magnus Enzensberger in einem Artikel über die „europäische Peripherie" fest: „Was die Arme Welt selber sagt, wird … kaum zur Notiz genommen. Ihre Wortführer und Theoretiker werden kaum übersetzt, noch weniger gelesen. Kwame Nkrumah gilt als ein öder Schreihals, Fidel Castro als bärtiger Schwätzer, Frantz Fanon, dessen Schriften auf die afrikanische und

asiatische Intelligenz einen enormen Einfluss üben, ist bei uns ein Unbekannter."[5]

Vier, fünf Jahre später mochte das Interesse an Intellektuellen der Dritten Welt wie Fanon oder Nkrumah in antiimperialistischen Kreisen in West-Berlin oder Frankfurt gewachsen sein. Doch selbst um 1970 war der Name Nkrumah wohl nur wenigen geläufig. Ganz zu schweigen von seiner dekolonialen politischen Ökonomie, die Gibbs und Norman mit erstaunlicher Entschlossenheit auf den Fernsehbildschirm brachten, zur Hauptsendezeit. Ob sich jemand Notizen gemacht hat?

Tom Holert

---

2 Der anfangs zitierte Satz aus *On Africa* dürfte sich auf diese Passage aus Nkrumahs Buch beziehen: „modern neo-colonialism is based upon the control of nominally independent States by giant financial interests. These interests often act through or on behalf of a particular capitalist State, but they are quite capable of acting on their own and forcing those imperial countries in which they have a dominant interest to follow their lead", (ebd., S. 22).

3 Ebd., S. 241.

4 Ebd., S. 220.

---

5 Hans Magnus Enzensberger, „Europäische Peripherie", in: *Kursbuch* 2, August 1965, S. 154–73, hier: S. 164.

Hidden Persuader

Ungefähr in der Mitte des Films *On Africa* fällt im Off zum ersten (aber nicht zum letzten) Mal der Begriff „Neo-Kolonialismus". Ein erster Definitionsversuch umreißt seine wesentlichen Konturen: „Neo-Kolonialismus ist die Kontrolle über formal unabhängige Staaten durch Gruppen des Großfinanzkapitals. Diese Gruppen werden von imperialistischen Regierungen unterstützt."

Die Worte werden über (oder neben) einem perkussiven Soundtrack und dem Anblick von (kurz aufflackernden) Fotografien einer Texaco-Tankstelle und vier Schnappschüssen von unscheinbaren, gewöhnlichen Gebäuden vorgetragen, die alle aus dem Fenster eines Autos aufgenommen wurden, das durch die Außenbezirke von Luanda fährt. Zwischen den Fotos erscheint der erste von insgesamt fünf Zwischentiteln, in Großbuchstaben: „NEO-KOLONIALISMUS".

In den folgenden etwa fünf Minuten erläutert die Off-Stimme das Thema, abwechselnd begleitet von Trommeln und anderen Geräuschen (von denen einige denen einer Registrierkasse ähneln) sowie weiteren Fotos von im Vorbeifahren geknipsten Straßenszenen, ergänzt durch Listen und Diagramme zu transnationalen Finanznetzwerken, präsentiert vor dem Hintergrund der Flaggen Großbritanniens, Frankreichs und der Bundesrepublik Deutschland.

Mit der Einführung des Begriffs „Neo-Kolonialismus" führt der Film auch einen seiner wichtigsten Theoretiker ein (wenn auch ohne dessen Namen zu nennen oder direkt auf seine Schriften zu verweisen). Offenbar hielten es Joey Gibbs und Skip Norman nicht für nötig, die Hauptquelle ihrer zentralen Konzepte, aber auch ihrer statistischen Daten und wörtlichen Formulierungen offen zu legen.

Denn dieser Teil von *On Africa* basiert auf Kwame Nkrumahs 1965 erschienenem Buch *Neo-Colonialism: The Last Stage of Imperialism*. Nkrumah, der erste Premierminister und Präsident des unabhängigen Ghana sowie ein antikolonialer Intellektueller und Politiker

par excellence, entwickelte und vermittelte seine panafrikanistische (und zunehmend sozialistische) Politik in einer Reihe umfassender Abhandlungen.

Ihm wird das Verdienst zugeschrieben, die erste grundlegende konzeptionelle Ausarbeitung des Neokolonialismus geliefert und den Begriff im Diskurs der antiimperialistischen und antikapitalistischen afrikanischen Linken verankert zu haben. Die wahrscheinlich am häufigsten zitierten Zeilen aus seinem Buch (die Gibbs und Norman jedoch auslassen) lauten: „Das Wesen des Neo-Kolonialismus besteht darin, dass der Staat, der ihm unterworfen ist, theoretisch unabhängig ist und alle äußeren Merkmale internationaler Souveränität besitzt. In Wirklichkeit jedoch wird sein Wirtschaftssystem und damit auch seine politische Politik von außen gelenkt."[1]

Obwohl Nkrumah weithin als Hauptautor angesehen wurde, blieb – nicht zuletzt in den Augen eben jener imperialistischen Kräfte, die er im Untertitel anprangerte – umstritten, ob er dieses Buch (und andere) tatsächlich selbst geschrieben hat. Nach einer längeren Periode in den 1950er- und frühen 1960er-Jahren, in der Ghana ein enger wirtschaftlicher Partner und politischer Verbündeter der Vereinigten Staaten gewesen war, begann Nkrumah seine Beziehungen zu den USA zu überdenken, bis zu dem Punkt, an dem er diese zu den gefährlichsten Akteuren des „Neo-Kolonialismus" erklärte. Zu den Auslösern dieses Sinneswandels gehörte maßgeblich die Ermordung seines kongolesischen Amtskollegen Patrice Lumumba im Jahr 1961 – ein Verbrechen, das zumindest teilweise von der CIA betrieben worden war.

Die Veröffentlichung des Buchs versetzte die amerikanische Diplomatie in Aufregung. Washington betrachtete Nkrumahs Angriffe mit großer Sorge, beklagte einen angeblich „zutiefst beunruhigenden und beleidigenden" antiamerikanischen Ton. Am 24. Februar 1966, drei Monate nachdem die Vereinigten Staaten ihre Empörung kundgetan hatten,

---

1 Kwame Nkrumah, *Neo-Colonialism: The Last Stage of Imperialism,* New York, 1965, S. ix.

Afrika aus Berlin

Der Titel ist eindeutig: ein Film über Afrika – den Kontinent, seine Ausbeutungs- und Gewaltgeschichte und seinen dekolonialen Kampf. Zugleich ist *On Africa* ein Film über West-Berlin, die Stadt, in die Skip Norman 1966 gezogen war. Die ersten Bilder sind schwarz-weiße Fahrtaufnahmen vom Kurfürstendamm. Sie sind als Negativ zu sehen, die weißen Passanten erscheinen schwarz. Die Kamerafahrt registriert die Geschäfte und Cafés, die Banken, das Kaufhaus des Westens, Orte des Konsums. Im Voice-over weist eine der beiden Frauenstimmen auf die wirtschaftliche Grundlage dieses Reichtums hin. „Die Erde Afrikas ist reich", sagt sie. „Ihre Produkte aber bereichern nicht die Afrikaner, sondern hauptsächlich immer noch Gruppen und Einzelne, die auf Afrikas Verarmung hinarbeiten." Von Anfang an sind wir mit einer Kluft zwischen Bild und Ton konfrontiert. Die Lücke weist strukturell auf die Asymmetrie zwischen den Kolonialmächten und ihren Opfern hin. Die Didaktik des Films nutzt oft solche Kontraste zwischen Gesagtem und Gesehenem.

Nach einer nüchternen Bilanz der extraktivistischen Ausbeutung des Kontinents kehren wir nach siebzehn Minuten nach Berlin zurück – diesmal in das Berlin von 1884. Schwarz-Weiß-Fotos zeigen ein luxuriöses Gebäude, das Reichskanzlerpalais, auch bekannt als „Alte Reichskanzlei". Heute existiert es nicht mehr, damals befand es sich in der Wilhelmstraße, nicht weit vom heutigen Standort der Deutschen Film- und Fernsehakademie Berlin (DFFB) am Potsdamer Platz. Zwischen dem 15. November 1884 und dem 26. Februar 1885 trafen sich hier die europäischen Kolonialmächte zur berüchtigten „Kongo-Konferenz", um den afrikanischen Kontinent in Einflusszonen aufzuteilen. Skip Normans Film zeigt dieses Ereignis als eine der Urszenen kolonialer Gewalt; mehr noch, es ist das politische Ereignis, an dem sich die beiden Triebkräfte des Westens, der Kolonialismus und der Imperialismus, in perfektem Einklang studieren lassen. Auf halber Strecke zwischen der brutalen Eroberung des Kontinents im 15. und 16. Jahrhundert und der zeitgenössischen Entwicklungspolitik um 1970 steht Berlin im Mittelpunkt der minutiös geplanten und durchgeführten Unterdrückung der afrikanischen Bevölkerung.

Zu den Bildern des Konsums und der Ausbeutung am Kurfürstendamm und der Konzentration auf einen der Hauptschauplätze europäischer Gewalt 1884/85 tritt der spezifische Hintergrund der DFFB. Skip Norman hatte dort 1969 mit *Strange Fruit* seinen Abschlussfilm gemacht. Offiziell war er kein Student mehr, als er *On Africa* realisierte. Die Stimmen im Film verweisen auf den Schulkontext. Die männliche Stimme gehört Klaus Wildenhahn, einem wichtigen Protagonisten des „direct cinema" in Deutschland. Wildenhahn hatte nach den Tumulten der Jahre 1967/68, die im Rauswurf von 18 Studenten mündeten, an der DFFB zu unterrichten begonnen. Auf Wildenhahns Initiative hin entstand ein neues Gemeinschaftsgefühl mit kollektiven Projekten wie der „Wochenschau". Eine der beiden Frauenstimmen ist die von Ingrid Oppermann, die 1970 an der DFFB zu studieren begann. Höchstwahrscheinlich stellte die Filmschule die Infrastruktur – den Tricktisch und andere Geräte – zur Verfügung, um den Film mit wenig Budget zu verwirklichen. Auch das Skript, das in dieser Broschüre abgedruckt ist, wurde in Skip Normans DFFB-Akte gefunden.

Zuletzt führt die Produktionsgeschichte von *On Africa* auch nach Ost-Berlin. Der Kameramann Resa Dabui erinnert sich, dass er und Skip Norman vom Osten der Stadt nach Luanda, Angola flogen. Eines der im Film enthaltenen Fotos zeigt die beiden am Flughafen. Als sie dort ankamen, saßen sie ohne Drehgenehmigung am Flughafen fest. Zu diesem Zeitpunkt drohte *On Africa* als Filmprojekt zu scheitern. Vermutlich wurde der Film am Schneidetisch der DFFB gerettet. Aber das ist eine andere Geschichte.

Volker Pantenburg

Ticken einer Uhr. In solchen Assoziationen zwischen Ton und Bild erweckt Norman den Eindruck, dass der Prozess des Geldzählens genauso unaufhaltsam weitergeht wie die Zeit. Die folgenden Bilder sind ein Echo und ein Kontrast zur ersten Szene des Films, in der wir Passanten in einer modernen Stadt in schwarz-weißem Negativ sehen. Jetzt zeigt Norman die andere Seite der Medaille, indem er die Gesichter und die Landschaft verfallener Orte in Afrika zeigt und so ein Bild derjenigen schafft, die von der Ausbeutung betroffen sind, die den Lebensstil der Menschen im globalen Norden finanziert, in diesem Fall in den Straßen von West-Berlin.

Der Neokolonialismus ist nicht auf den afrikanischen Kontinent beschränkt. Er dehnt sich auf Asien und Lateinamerika aus, oft getarnt als „Hilfe". Norman verbindet den Neokolonialismus mit Lumumbas letztem Brief, in dem er den internationalen Kampf für die Befreiung verkündet: „Wir sind nicht allein. Afrika, Asien und die freien und befreiten Völker in der ganzen Welt werden immer auf der Seite der Millionen Kongolesen zu finden sein, die den Kampf nicht vor dem Tag aufgeben werden." Normans Zusammenstellung von „Gegenerinnerungen"[2] und seine Lektion über Befreiung und ihre Hindernisse, die aus fragmentierten Bildern und Klängen besteht, erinnert uns an Eshuns Ausgrabungsstätte, an den Ort, von dem aus die Befreiungskämpfe gedacht werden können. Es ist eine eindrucksvolle visuelle Lektion darüber, was getan werden muss, um die Arbeit fortzusetzen, für die die Befreiungsbewegungen auf der ganzen Welt täglich kämpfen.

„Kein Land Afrikas wurde unabhängig ohne Opfer (und) keinem Land wurde die Unabhängigkeit geschenkt". Mit diesen Worten eröffnet Norman in *On Africa* das Kapitel über „Befreiung". Begleitet von Explosions- und Schussgeräuschen versetzt Norman uns auf die Bühne des Befreiungskrieges – ein Weg, den viele Bewegungen gewählt haben, um die im Kampf gegen den Kolonialismus gesteckten Ziele zu erreichen. Die Schlussbilder des Films zeigen Moise Tshombe (1919–1969) und Patrice Lumumba, wobei ersterer die Zerstörung des Kongo und die Allianz mit den Kolonialmächten verkörpert, während letzterer von den Kolonialmächten „eingesperrt" und ermordet wurde. Es ist der Herzschlag, der Lumumbas Brief begleitet, in dem seine letzten Worte stehen: „Lang lebe Afrika!"

Sónia Vaz Borges

---

2 Ebd., S. 288.

Fragmente für die Zukunft der Befreiung rekonstruieren

In „Further Considerations on Afrofuturism" spekuliert Kodwo Eshun über eine zukünftige Generation afrikanischer Archäolog*innen, die auf eine Ausgrabungsstätte stoßen. Sie finden zerstörte Dokumente, die zu unserer Gegenwart gehören, und das Staunen regt uns an, „uns vorzustellen, wie sie den konzeptionellen Rahmen unseres kulturellen Moments aus diesen Fragmenten rekonstruieren".[1]

Skip Normans *On Africa* lässt uns daran denken, dass die Zukunft, die Eshun uns vorzustellen vorschlägt, vor uns liegt, aber auch aus der Vergangenheit geerbt werden kann. Die sechsunddreißig Minuten Film konfrontieren uns mit einer Sammlung von Bildern und Tönen, die nicht unbedingt einer historischen Chronologie folgen, sondern Zukünfte hervorbringen und die Plattform für einen Aufbruch bieten.

Die letzten Worte des ersten Premierministers der Demokratischen Republik Kongo, Patrice Lumumba (1925–1961), in einem Brief an Pauline Lumumba und ihre Kinder (der aber genauso gut an alle Afrikaner*innen und die Diaspora gerichtet sein könnte), prophezeien eine besondere afrikanische Zukunft: „Die Geschichte wird es eines Tages berichten, aber nicht die Geschichte, die in Brüssel gelehrt wird, sondern die Geschichte, die in den vom Imperialismus und seinen Marionetten befreiten Ländern gelehrt wird. Afrika wird seine eigene Geschichte schreiben und nördlich und südlich der Sahara wird es eine ruhmreiche und würdige Geschichte sein."

Dieses „Recht auf ein ehrenvolles Leben, auf unbefleckte Würde und auf uneingeschränkte Unabhängigkeit" war dank verschiedener Kollektive und internationalistischer Bewegungen auf dem Kontinent bereits im Entstehen begriffen. FRELIMO in Mosambik, SWAPO in Namibia, PAIGC in Guinea-Bissau und Cabo Verde, MPLA in Angola, der ANC in Südafrika und ZAPU in Simbabwe sind einige der Organisationen, die Norman anführt, um uns die Geografie der Befreiung von Imperialismus, Kapitalismus, Kolonialismus und Neokolonialismus vorzustellen.

Der Befreiungskampf ist ein kollektiver Kampf, dessen Ziel über die Unabhängigkeit hinausgeht. Er ist eine individuelle/kollektive, prozesshafte Reaktion der Menschen, die sich der Rassifizierung, Entmenschlichung, Unterdrückung und Ausbeutung bewusstwerden, durch die sie unter der kolonial-oppressiven Regierung innerhalb und außerhalb ihres „Landes" geknechtet werden. Sie organisieren sich, um die Struktur der Unterdrückung abzubauen und zu zerstören, um ihre Souveränität und „Gerechtigkeit und Würde" als freie Menschen aufzubauen, wobei die Unabhängigkeit, in den Worten Lumumbas, ein entscheidender Übergang zur Befreiung der Zukunft ist.

Die Vision einer befreiten Zukunft Afrikas und der Afrikaner*innen kann nicht entstehen, ohne zu zeigen, wie die Geografien der Unterdrückung den Raum weltweit beherrschen; wie sie zu allen Zeiten und an allen Orten verbreitet und weiterentwickelt werden, und ein internationales Netzwerk von Gewalt und Entmenschlichung bilden. Durch die Währung und die sieben Währungszonen in Afrika werden die Verbindungen zu den ehemaligen Kolonialmächten fortgeschrieben. Ab Minute 21:53, im Abschnitt über „Neo-Kolonialismus", zeigt Norman, wie sich Kolonialismus und Imperialismus in einer schwer nachzeichenbaren Struktur entwickelt haben, die die Gründung einer Afrikanischen Wirtschaftsgemeinschaft oder, wenn wir Eshuns afrofuturistische Vision aufgreifen wollen, der Vereinigten Staaten von Afrika – USAF, verhindert.

Norman stellt diese Struktur nicht nur schematisch dar, sondern verbindet Klänge mit visuellen Effekten: Dia-Bilder von Banken ziehen in schneller Folge vorbei. Der Rhythmus ist mit Klickgeräuschen verbunden, die an eine Banknotenzählmaschine oder eine Registrierkasse erinnern, kombiniert mit dem

---

1 Kodwo Eshun, "Further Considerations on Afrofuturism," in: *CR: The New Centennial Review*, Bd. 3, Nr. 2, Sommer 2003, S. 287–302, hier S. 287.

Material

Der letzte Brief von Patrice Lumumba an seine Frau, kurz vor seiner Ermordung
im Januar 1961.

Meine liebe Frau!

Während ich diese Zeilen schreibe, weiß ich nicht, ob sie Dich erreichen werden, wenn sie
zu Dir gelangen werden und ob ich noch am Leben bin, wenn Du sie liest. Während
meines Kampfes für die Unabhängigkeit meines Landes habe ich nie einen einzigen Augen-
blick daran gezweifelt, daß die heilige Sache, der meine Gefährten und ich unser ganzes
Leben gewidmet haben, schließlich triumphieren wird. Aber was wir unserem Land gewünscht
haben – sein Recht auf ein ehrenvolles Leben, auf unbefleckte Würde und auf uneingeschränkte Unabhängigkeit –, haben die belgischen Imperialisten und die westlichen Alliierten
niemals gewollt. Sie haben unmittelbare und mittelbare Unterstützung von gewissen
hohen Beamten der Vereinten Nationen – sowohl bewußt als auch unbewußt – erhalten,
während wir dieser Organisation völlig vertrauten, als wir sie um Hilfe baten.

Sie haben einige unserer Gefährten korrumpiert, andere bestochen. Sie haben dabei ge-
holfen die Wahrheit zu verzerren und unsere Unabhänigkeit in Verruf zu bringen. Wie
könnte ich anders reden? Tot oder lebendig, in Freiheit oder im Gefängnis auf Anordnung
der Imperialisten – nicht ich bin wichtig. Wichtig ist der Kongo, ist unser armes Volk,
dessen Unabhängigkeit in einen Käfig verwandelt wurde, durch dessen Gitter uns die Welt
draußen betrachtet, manchmal mit freundlichem Mitleid, aber auch mit Freude und Gefallen.

Mein Glaube jedoch wird unerschüttert bleiben. Ich weiß und fühle es in meinem Herzen,
daß mein Volk sich früher oder später von all seinen inneren und äußeren Feinden befreien
und sich wie ein Mann erheben wird, um „Nein" zu der Erniedrigung und Schande des
Kolonialismus zu sagen und seine Würde im klaren Licht der Sonne wiederzugewinnen.
Wir sind nicht allein. Afrika, Asien und die freien und befreiten Völker in der ganzen Welt
werden immer auf der Seite der Millionen Kongolesen zu finden sein, die den Kampf
nicht vor dem Tag aufgeben werden, an dem es keine Kolonialisten und Söldner in unserem
Land gibt. Ich möchte, daß meinen Kindern, die ich verlasse und vielleicht nie wieder
sehe, gesagt wird, daß es ihre Pflicht wie die jedes Kongolesen ist, die heilige Aufgabe zu
vollbringen, unsere Unabhängigkeit und Souveränität wiederzuerrichten: denn ohne
Gerechtigkeit keine Würde und ohne Unabhängigkeit keine freien Menschen.

Weder Brutalität, Grausamkeit noch Folter wird mich jemals dazu bringen, um Gnade zu
flehen, denn ich sterbe lieber mit ungebeugtem Haupt, unerschütterlichem Glauben und
tiefem Vertrauen in das Schicksal meines Landes, als unterjocht leben und heilige Grund-
sätze verleugnen zu müssen. Die Geschichte wird es eines Tages berichten, aber nicht die
Geschichte, die in Brüssel gelehrt wird, sondern die Geschichte, die in den vom Imperialismus
und seinen Marionetten befreiten Ländern gelehrt wird. Afrika wird seine eigene Geschichte schreiben und nördlich und südlich der Sahara wird es eine ruhmreiche und würdige
Geschichte sein. Weine nicht um mich, meine liebe Frau. Ich bin sicher, daß mein Land,
das so viel leidet, weiß, wie es seine Unabhängigkeit und seine Freiheit verteidigen muß.

Lang lebe der Kongo! Lang lebe Afrika!

Patrice

Dokument

ist nicht durch Verhandlung oder Kompromiß, sondern allein im revolutionären Kampf durchzusetzen.

Stimme 1

Kein Land Afrikas wurde unabhängig ohne Opfer. Alle Konzessionen seitens der Imperialisten wurden durch die Aktionen der Massen erzwungen. Keinem Land wurde die Unabhängigkeit geschenkt.

Die Imperialisten haben zwei Hauptziele in Afrika:

1) zu sichern, daß die Länder, die ihre Unabhängigkeit errungen haben, weiter unter imperialistischer Beherrschung bleiben.

2) Portugals und Südafrikas unmenschliche Ausbeutung der Bevölkerung und Reichtümer des südlichen Afrikas zu festigen und diese Territorien als ein Bollwerk der weißen Herrschaft in Afrika zu benutzen.

Stimme 2

Afrika ist Land. Der Kampf um Verbesserung der Landwirtschaft und ländlichen Entwicklung wird die Zukunft des Kontinents und der einzelnen Nationen entscheiden.

Es ist notwendig, die genauen Verhältnisse der landwirtschaftlichen Entwicklung und des industriellen Aufbaus festzustellen und zu ermitteln.

Industrialisierung muß mit den Notwendigkeiten und Möglichkeiten der eigenen Wirtschaft zusammenhängen und kann nicht im Hinblick auf Befriedigung der europäischen Gesellschaften geschehen. Sie darf nicht von den Prinzipien, die aus den materialistischen Gesellschaften der industriellen Supermächte resultiert, gelenkt werden.

```
FRELIMO ----------- MOZAMBIQUE
MPLA --------------- ANGOLA
PAIGC -------------- GUINEA BISSAU
SWAPO -------------- SOUTHWEST AFRICA
ANC ---------------- SOUTH AFRICA
ZAPU --------------- ZIMBABWE
```

Dokument

Dokument

Stimme 1

Eine der effektivsten Methoden der Imperialisten, ökonomische
Herrschaft über die ehemaligen Kolonialgebiete aufrechtzuerhalten,
ist zu versuchen, daß die jungen Staaten in den Geldzonen der
imperialistischen Finanzzentren eingeschränkt bleiben.
Es gibt 7 Hauptwährungsgruppen in Afrika:
die französische Franczone,

Dokumentation
über den
Neo-Kolonialismus

die englische Sterlingzone,
die belgische Franczone,
die spanische Pesetazone,
die portugiesische Escudozone
und andere Länder wie die Vereinigte Arabische Republik und
der Kongo (Kinshasa) mit anderen Währungseinheiten.
Der größte Teil des Handels in Afrika ist in der Sterlingzone
und der französischen Franczone.

Das Vorhandensein einzelner Geldzonen verursacht einen schäd-
lichen Effekt bei dem Zuwachs des Handels in Afrika und
führt zu illegalem Handel und Einkommensverlusten in vielen
Ländern. Es verhindert den Aufbau einer afrikanischen Wirtschaftsgemeinschaft. Diese Geldzonen setzen die Verbindungen
mit den ehemaligen kolonialen Mächten fort und verstärken
die Kräfte des Neo-Kolonialismus.

Stimme 2

Eine andere Methode des Neo-Kolonialismus ist die Benutzung
hoher Zinssätze. Zahlen der Weltbank von 1962 zeigen, daß
71 Länder aus Asien, Afrika und Lateinamerika ungefähr 27 Mrd.
Auslandsschulden hatten, wofür sie außerdem etwa 5 Mrd. Dollar
in Zinsen und Dienstleistungen bezahlen mußten.

Stimme 3

1961 z.B. betrug der Profit an internationaler Hilfe 5 Mrd. Dollar,
an Zinsen 1 Mrd. und an nicht äquivalentem Austausch

Fotomontage
Metropole –
Kolonialstadt

5,8 Mrd. – d.h. eine Gesamtzahl von 11,8 Mrd., die gegen eine
Investition von 6 Mrd. Dollar gewonnen wurden. Also ist „Hilfe"
nicht mehr als eine andere Methode der Ausbeutung, eine
moderne Methode kapitalistischen Exports – nur mit einem
anderen Namen.

Die Freiheits-
bewegung:
Training
Studium
Produktion

BEFREIUNG   Stimme 3

Die „Rückkehr der afrikanischen Völker zur Geschichte" setzt
die Befreiung des Entwicklungsprozesses der nationalen Produktiv-
kräfte von jeder Art imperialistischer Herrschaft voraus und

Dokument

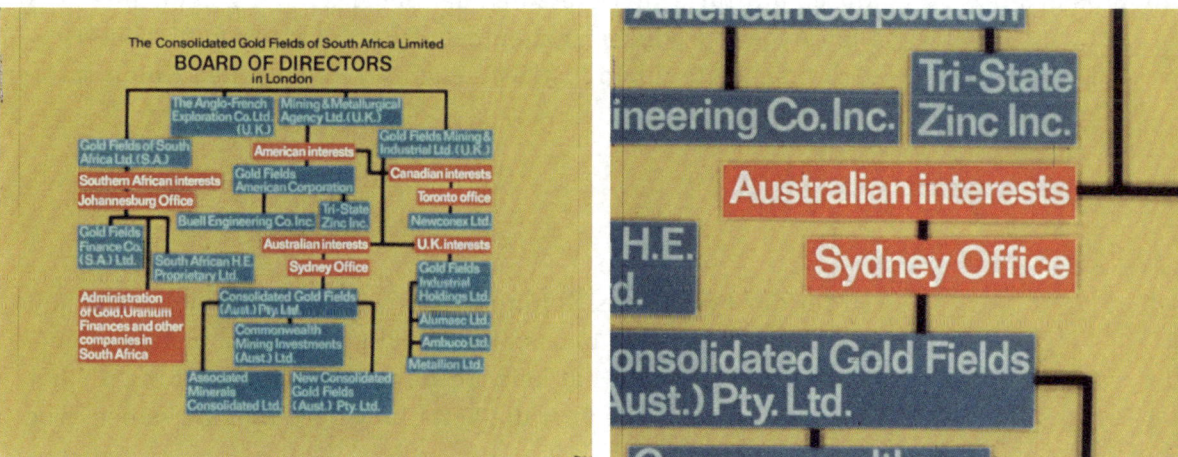

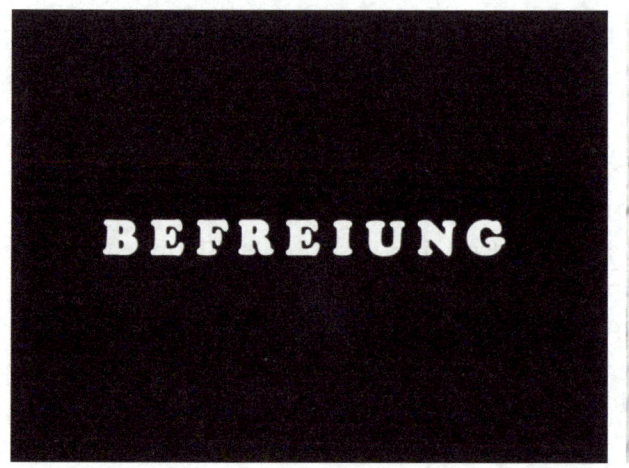 

Dokument

KOLONIALISMUS   Stimme 1

Dokumentation des
Kolonialismus

Kolonialismus – die Unterjochung von Territorien und Völkern
durch militärische Besetzung, um Bodenschätze zu gewinnen und
sich Arbeitsprodukte anzueignen. Diese Territorien dienen als
Arbeitsmärkte für Industrieerzeugnisse, die von den Kolonisatoren
kommen.

(Motiv)

Stimme 2

Unter der Politik des Kolonialismus wird das kolonialisierte Volk
als bloßes Werkzeug betrachtet. Es ist gezwungen, in äußerster
Armut zu leben und hat kein Recht auf Selbstverwaltung. Es hat
auch keine Kontrolle über die Verteilung der Produkte seiner Arbeit.

(Motiv)

Das Resultat –
Äußerste Armut in den Kolonien war die Basis
des Reichtums und Luxus in Europa.

(Motiv)

NEO-KOLONIALISMUS   Stimme 1

Neo-Kolonialismus ist die Kontrolle über formal unabhängige
Staaten durch Gruppen des Großfinanzkapitals. Diese Gruppen
werden von imperialistischen Regierungen unterstützt.

(Motiv)

Stimme 3

Statistische
Daten

1957 liefert Afrika Europa folgende Menge von Grundstoffen
für ihre Industrien.

Stimme 3

Dokumentarische
Bilder

Die U.S.A. sind einer der Hauptvertreter des Neo-Kolonialismus.
Zwischen 1950 und 1959 investierten private amerikanische
Firmen 4,5 Mrd. Dollar in die Entwicklungsländer. Sie machten
einen Gewinn, der dreimal größer war als die Investitionen.
Nettoprofite lagen bei 8,3 Mrd. Dollar, hinzu kommen Millionen
von Handelsprofiten, Zinsen auf Anleihen, Frachtgebühren
und Gewinne aus anderen Geschäften.

Dokument

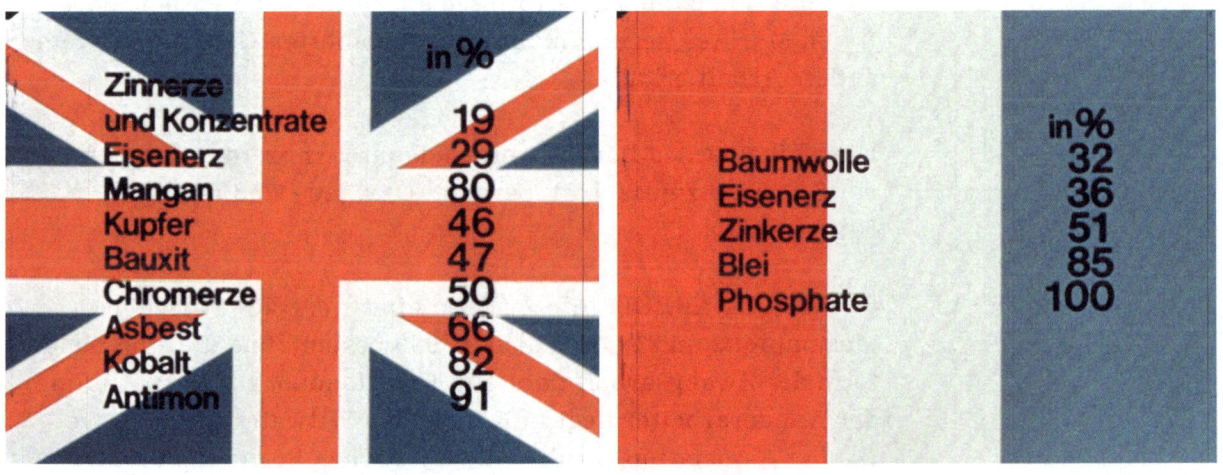

Zinnerze	in %
und Konzentrate	19
Eisenerz	29
Mangan	80
Kupfer	46
Bauxit	47
Chromerze	50
Asbest	66
Kobalt	82
Antimon	91

	in %
Baumwolle	32
Eisenerz	36
Zinkerze	51
Blei	85
Phosphate	100

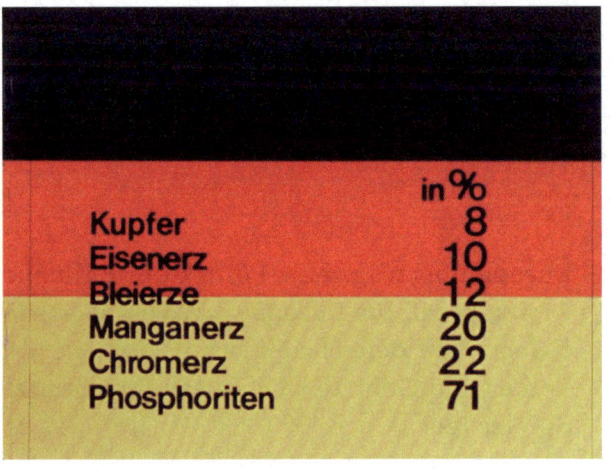

	in %
Kupfer	8
Eisenerz	10
Bleierze	12
Manganerz	20
Chromerz	22
Phosphoriten	71

5) ZWANGSANBAU von Baumwolle. In Nordmozambique schreiben zwölf Kompanien, die das Monopol in diesem Gebiet besitzen, den afrikanischen Bauern den Anbau von Baumwolle vor. Diese muß die Kompanie zu Festpreisen abgeben, die unter denen des freien Marktes liegen. In den konzessionierten Gebieten ist keine andere Arbeit erlaubt.

Die afrikanischen Bauern werden dadurch ihrer Existenzgrundlage, der Subsistenzwirtschaft, beraubt. Die Folge sind häufige Hungersnöte.

6) WANDERARBEIT, die in Form eines Vertrags zwischen Mozambique und Transvaal seit 1909 besteht, und die eine Sonderform der Zwangsarbeit darstellt. Das Monopol zur Rekrutierung der Wanderarbeiter liegt in Händen der Witwatersrand Native Labour Association, die der portugiesischen Regierung pro Arbeiter 1 Pfund 18 s zahlt.

Die Folge: eine intensive Ausbeutung Afrikas durch den Sklavenhandel, um eine gigantische Arbeitskraft für Europas Produktion und gesellschaftlichen Fortschritt auszunutzen.

Stimme 3

Europa 1800

Europa übertrug seine Politik der Balkanisierung auf Afrika. Afrika besaß für Europa so großen Wert, daß es seinetwegen zu Kriegen auf dem europäischen Kontinent kommen mußte. Völker und Gebiete wechselten ihre Besitzer wie Kinder ihre Spielzeuge.

So kam es, daß die große Berliner Konferenz der Imperialisten und Kolonialisten im November 1884 – Januar 1885 stattfand, um Lösungen für die Aufteilung von Territorien entlang der Atlantikküste und in Zentralafrika zu finden.

Sie verursachte Konflikte zwischen den europäischen Staaten, die zur Zerstückelung Afrikas in Einflußgebiete der europäischen Nationen führte.

1890 wurden die deutschen und englischen Einflußgebiete festgelegt und der Weg freigemacht für ein stärkeres Eindringen sowie für eine verschärfte Ausbeutung der Bodenschätze im Kongotiefland und der großen Mineralfundstätten weiter südlich.

(Motiv)

Dokument

Dokument

steht an zweiter Stelle der afrikanischen Sisalproduktion

an fünfter Stelle der Erdölproduktion in Afrika

Fotomontage portugiesischer Wohlstand Angola gegenüber (Didaktik)

wird in wenigen Jahren einen Platz unter den ersten drei einnehmen

an sechster Stelle der afrikanischen Tabakerzeugung

ist größter afrikanischer Papierproduzent

steht an zweiter Stelle bei der Gewinnung von Diamanten auf dem afrikanischen Kontinent

ist zweitgrößter Erzlieferant Afrikas und liegt an zwölfter Stelle der Weltproduktion.

Stimme 2

Portugiesischer Wohlstand

Portugal betreibt die extremste und primitivste Art der Ausbeutung, die in Afrika existiert.
Nach dem 1828 erlassenen Arbeitsgesetz für Eingeborene, das im wesentlichen noch heute gültig ist, kann man sechs Formen der Ausbeutung einheimischer Arbeitskraft in den portugiesischen Kolonien unterscheiden.

1) ZWANGSARBEIT bei der Übertretung von Strafe oder Arbeitsgesetzen, z.B. bei Nichtbezahlung der Kopfsteuer.

2) PFLICHTARBEIT, die jedem auferlegt werden kann, wenn für öffentliche Arbeiten nicht genügend Arbeiter vorhanden sind. Ausnahme: Kinder unter 14 Jahre, Erwachsene über 60 Jahre, Kranke und Invalide, anerkannte Häuptlinge, Afrikaner mit ständiger Anstellung.

3) VERTRAGSARBEIT als ökonomisch wichtigste Form der Zwangsarbeit in den portugiesischen Kolonien. Jeder Afrikaner, dem es nicht gelingt, nachzuweisen, daß er während mindestens 6 Monate des vergangenen Jahres in einem Arbeitsverhältnis war, kann zur Zwangsarbeit für den Staat oder für private Unternehmer herangezogen werden.

4) FREIWILLIGE ARBEIT, bei der die Arbeiter direkt mit dem Unternehmer einen Vertrag abschließen, der den afrikanischen Arbeitern als einzigen Vorteil gegenüber der Vertragsarbeit einen Arbeitsplatz in der Nähe ihres Dorfes gewährleistet. Die Löhne für Freiwillige Arbeit sind im Durchschnitt noch niedriger als die für Vertragsarbeit.

Dokument

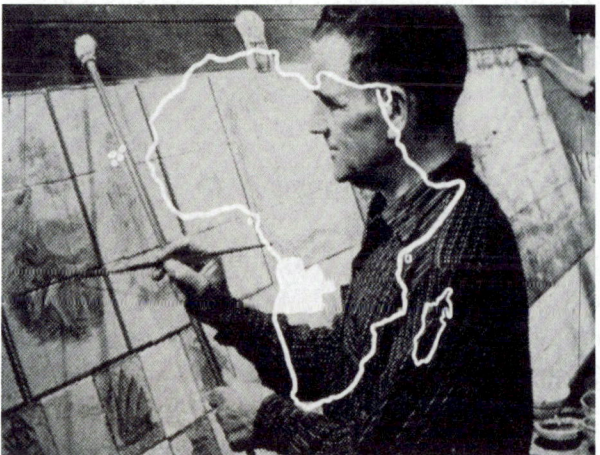

Dokument

Stimme 3

Imperialismus – Europas Ausbreitung der kapitalistischen
Ausbeutung und Verbreitung von Christentum und Rassentheorien
über mehr als die Hälfte der Menschheit.

REPEAT: Stimme 1

Stimme 3

Imperialismus – Europas unmenschliche Erfindung von Konzen-
trationslagern, Massenverstümmelung und Massenmord,
Schändung von Frauen, gräßliche Behandlung von Kindern,
die Zerstörung von Kulturen überall in der Welt.

Stimme 1

Imperialismus – Europas unmenschliche Erfindung von Konzen-
trationslagern, Massenverstümmelung und Massenmord,
Schändung von Frauen, gräßliche Behandlung von Kindern,
die Zerstörung von Kulturen überall in der Welt, das alles im Namen
und für die Verteidigung einer Rassentheorie. Mit einer Über-
legenheit der europäischen christlichen Zivilisation, die sich dafür
ausersehen fühlt, die Welt zu regieren.

Stimme 3

Europäer
in Afrika

Nachdem Europa seine sogenannte „Neue Welt" entdeckt hatte,
führte es das verhängnisvolle System der dauerhaften Sklaverei
ein. Es entstand eine neue Doktrin der Arbeit. Die Menschen
wurden in zwei Klassen eingeteilt: die Herrenmenschen und die
Untermenschen, die Herrenmenschen waren die wirklichen
Menschen, die Untermenschen aber nur Halbmenschen oder sogar
noch weniger.

(Kirchenszene)

Sklaverei

So begann das erste Eindringen, die erste Zerstörung und Verwüs-
tung Afrikas, die Grundlage für die Entwicklung des Kapitalismus
in Europa.

Was ist Angola? Stimme 1

Afrika Karte IV
(schwarz – weiß)

Angola ist: der größte afrikanische Kaffeeproduzent und steht
an dritter Stelle der Weltproduktion

der zweitgrößte afrikanische Produzent von Fischmehl und Fischöl
und nimmt in der Weltproduzentenliste den zehnten Platz ein

Dokument

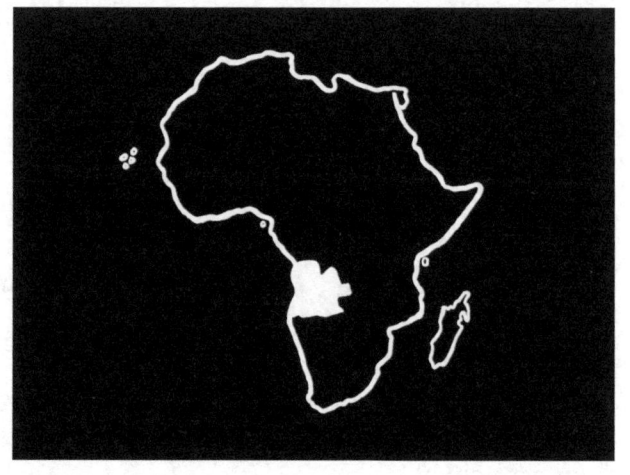

Dokument

Afrika besitzt mehr als 40 % der potentiellen Wasserkraft
der Welt, einen größeren Anteil als irgendein anderer Kontinent.
Davon wird aber nicht einmal 5 % genutzt.

(Geräusch von marschierenden Soldaten)

Trotz ausgedehnter Wüstenstrecken der Sahara hat Afrika
immer noch mehr Acker und Weideland als die U.S.A. oder
die Sowjetunion oder Asien.

Afrika Karte II   Afrika hat zweimal soviele Wälder wie die U.S.A.
(rosa – schwarz)

Stimme 3

Fahrt wird   Wenn Afrikas vielfältige Reichtümer für seine eigene Entwicklung
fortgesetzt   genutzt werden, so kann es zu dem modernsten Kontinent der
                    Welt zählen. Seine Reichtümer wurden und werden immer noch
                    für die größere Entwicklung von Auslandsinteressen benutzt.

                    Als Europa Afrika in seiner ganzen Größe, Stärke und Potenz
                    erkannte, hatte Afrika sich selbst längst so begriffen. Es hatte
                    seine eigenen Staatsformen und gesellschaftlichen Organisationen
                    entwickelt, die fest in seine Tradition verwurzelt und durch
                    seine Verschiedenartigkeit geprägt waren.

Afrika Karte III   Damals bestand die Welt aus vielen isolierten Kulturen, die sich
(rot – schwarz)   nach ihrer eigenen Dynamik entwickelten. Bis dann Europa seinen
Zerstückelung   Rahmen sprengte und eine Flut von Blut und unermeßlicher
Afrikas   Zerstörung hinterließ.

(Kriegsgeräusche)

IMPERIALISMUS   Stimme 2

Europa zuhause   Imperialismus ist die Praxis eines stärkeren Landes, seinen Willen
und in Afrika –   einem anderen Land durch militärische Gewalt aufzuzwingen,
Aristokratie –   um die ökonomische und politische Beherrschung dieses Volkes
Militär   zu erreichen.

                    REPEAT: Stimme 1

7

Dokument

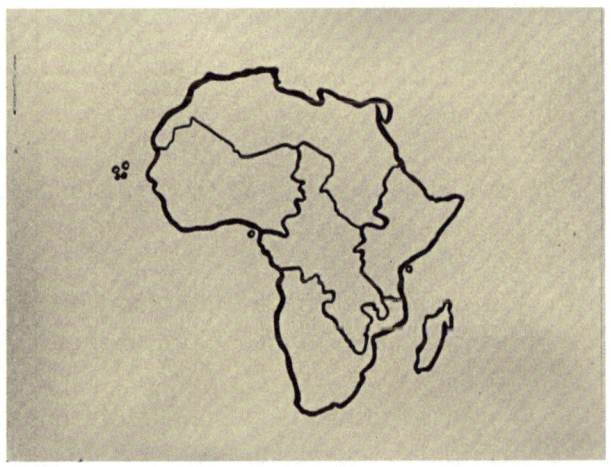

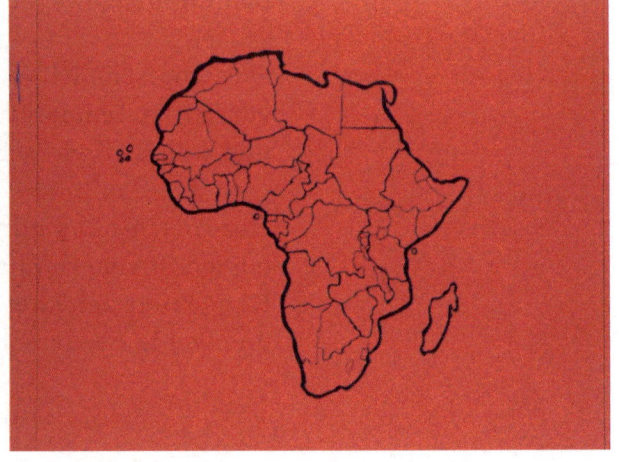

Dokument

Einleitung: Stimme 1

In Afrika unterscheidet man zwischen äquatorialem und
tropischem Klima.

Daneben gibt es noch mehrere kleine charakteristische
Klimazonen.

Fahrt an
Fußgängern
vorbei
(Negativeffekt)

Zentralafrika, Guinea und Ostafrika gehören zum
äquatorialen Klima.

In Guinea und Ostafrika findet man eine konstante Wärme
und eine geringere Niederschlagsmenge.

Sowohl im äquatorialen als auch im tropischen Klima gibt
es eine üppige Vegetation.

Das ostafrikanische Klima ist heiß. Es gibt Savanne und
mannigfaltige Vegetation.

Das tropische Klima unterteilt man in die sudanesische Art
von Hitze, Temperaturschwankungen zwischen Tag und Nacht
und wenig Niederschlag.

Darüber hinaus gibt es das typische Mittelmeerklima mit
heißen Sommern und Regen im Winter. Und das Klima des
Kapgebiets zeichnet sich durch mildere Sommer und Winter
und wenig Niederschlag aus.

(Tropisches Geräusch)

Stimme 2

Afrika Karte I
(weiß – schwarz)

Die Erde Afrikas ist reich. Ihre Produkte aber bereichern nicht
die Afrikaner, sondern hauptsächlich immer noch Gruppen und
Einzelne, die auf Afrikas Verarmung hinarbeiten.

Mit einer Bevölkerung von rund 280 Mill. Menschen, ungefähr
8 % der Weltbevölkerung, hat Afrika einen Anteil von nur 2 %
des gesamten Weltprodukts.

Fahrt wird
fortgesetzt

Man schätzt die Eisenvorräte Afrikas doppelt so hoch wie die
der U.S.A. und 2/3 die der Sowjetunion.

Afrikas berechnete Kohlenreserven reichen für 300 Jahre.

Neue Erdölvorkommen werden überall auf dem Kontinent gefunden und ausgebeutet. Die Verarbeitung aber von den
wichtigsten Erzen und Mineralien ist nur im Anfangsstadium.

Dokument

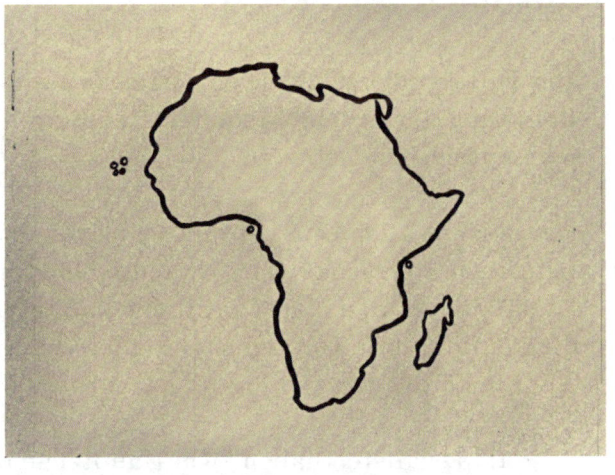

Dokument

<u>On Africa</u>
von Skip Norman

Der Dokumentarfilm *On Africa*, eine Co-produktion der Pan-African Arts CO-OP und Denso Film Berlin von Skip Norman und seinem Kameraden Joey Gibbs (Buch), handelt von den afrikanischen Befreiungskämpfen, die in Afrika heute geführt werden.

Der Ausgangspunkt dieses Films ist das Verhältnis zwischen Europas Wohlstand und Afrikas Armut; Europas Zerstörung von Gesellschaften und Kulturen und gleichzeitiger Einsatz von Christentum und Rassentheorien als Rechtfertigung einer gewaltigen Ausbeutung der Kolonialisierten.

Er zeigt durch eine dynamische Verbindung von Filmtechnik und Partisanenempfindungsvermögen in der Bearbeitung der Fakten die Stärke und Schwäche Europas als Folge des Kolonialalters: die Schwäche und Stärke Afrikas als Beweis für die Wiedergeburt Afrikas.

Der Fall <u>Angola</u> zeigt die europäische Meinung gegenüber der Befreiung Afrikas, insbesondere den Befreiungskämpfen in den portugiesischen Gebieten.

Heute ist es allen klar erkennbar, wie die europäischen Kolonialisten ihre Herrschaft in Afrika aufgebaut haben.
Es ist allen klar, daß das westliche kapitalistische System durch die Manipulation von Industrie- und Finanzkapital die Fortschritte Afrikas behindert.

„Die Imperialisten haben zwei Hauptziele in Afrika:

1) zu sichern, daß die Länder, die ihre Unabhängigkeit errungen haben, weiter unter imperialistischer Beherrschung bleiben.

2) Portugals und Südafrikas unmenschliche Ausbeutung der Bevölkerung und Reichtümer des südlichen Afrikas zu festigen und diese Territorien als ein Bollwerk der weißen Herrschaft in Afrika zu benutzen."

Der Film lässt den bewaffneten Kampf als den wahren Kampf erscheinen.
MPLA in Angola, FRELIMO in Mozambique, PAIGC in Guinea (Bissau), ZAPU in Zimbabwe (Südrhodesien), ANC in Azania (Südafrika) und SWAPO in Namibia (Südwestafrika) zeigen, daß der bewaffnete Kampf die Seelen und Energie des Volkes befreit.

Der letzte Brief Patrice Lumumbas an seine Frau beantwortet alle skeptischen Fragen.

Dokument

stimmen
    Ingrid Oppermann
    Li Antes
    Klaus Wildenhahn

ON AFRICA

buch
    Joey Gibbs
    Skip Norman

Inhalt

Dokument

Skip Norman: *On Africa* – Skript: S. 3

Material

Der letzte Brief von Patrice Lumumba an seine Frau, kurz vor seiner Ermordung
im Januar 1961: S. 21

Kommentar

Sónia Vaz Borges: Fragmente für die Zukunft der Befreiung rekonstruieren: S. 23

Volker Pantenburg: Afrika aus Berlin: S. 25

Tom Holert: Hidden Persuader: S. 26

Madeleine Bernstorff: Paratexte / (nachträgliche) Skripte oder
„Der letzte Brief Patrice Lumumbas an seine Frau beantwortet alle skeptischen Fragen.": S. 28

Marie-Hélène Gutberlet: Improvisationsmuster: S. 29

Editorische Notiz: S. 31

Impressum/Dank: S. 32

HaFI 018

Skip Norman:
On Africa

Dokument
Material
Kommentar